CHAGALL

Michel Makarius

Translated by Jane Brenton

STUDIO EDITIONS

LONDON

Originally published by Fernand Hazan, Paris 1986

This edition published 1988 by Studio Editions Ltd.
Princess House, 50 Eastcastle Street
London W1N 7AP, England

Reprinted 1988, 1990

ISBN 1-85170-148-6

Printed and bound in Hong Kong

After a journey lasting many days the young Chagall arrived at the Gare du Nord in Paris late in the summer of 1910. He was twenty-three, he had no money, and his luggage consisted only of a few paintings and drawings he had brought with him from Russia. All he knew was that he wanted to paint, unconstrained, free of academic restrictions and preconceived ideas. At first he felt bewildered and nearly succumbed to panic. How could it be otherwise? A young man steps down from a train and finds himself in the city of his dreams, a vast unfamiliar place. He speaks only Russian and Yiddish, and he comes from Vitebsk, a small town in the most westerly of the Russian provinces, on the frontier with Poland and the Baltic states.

The budding artist was not entirely inexperienced in the ways of the world. He had spent a year in St Petersburg under Léon Bakst, famous for his association with Diaghilev's *Ballets Russes*, and there he had rubbed shoulders with the intellectuals of his day. But above all he had found himself in the company of like-minded young men, and had shared with them his dreams of the irresistible Mecca that was Paris. It was a time for him of preparation, a gathering of forces for the leap into the unknown. His true initiation into the artist's life was not to occur until he was alone in foreign land, isolated from the familiar sights and sounds of his native country.

Such an adventure could have foundered at the start, were it not that Paris, uniquely, offered the conditions in which such bold spirits could survive, and even flourish. Paris, or more precisely, Montparnasse. For to this cramped quarter of the city flooded impoverished and ambitious young men from all over the world, fired by nothing more than a burning desire to pursue their artistic destiny. The legend of Montparnasse needs no repetition, yet it is only by understanding something of the life of the *Montparnos* that one can begin to comprehend how Chagall,

in spite of all the difficulties, was able to bury himself in work and produce, in his first few months, masterpieces like *Mazin, The Poet* and *The Drunkard*. For once the myth does not outstrip the reality. And that is not because accounts of the contemporary scene were unusually honest or objective. It is rather because the social context was one almost unimaginable to us today. For the price of a coffee, for example, you could spend the whole day in a café like the Dôme; at the restaurant where you ate regularly, and where your table-napkin was stored in its own place in the rack, credit was extended as a matter of course, or a drawing would be accepted as payment for the price of a meal; you could even rent a room for a trifling sum. It was above all because life was cheap that struggling artists found fame in Montparnasse. It was a poor area, away from the Left Bank, and its occupants rarely ventured much further afield. Everyone knew everyone else; familiarity inevitably led to gossip, and anecdotes spread like wildfire – usually with more than a little basis of fact behind them. It is largely for this reason that we are so well informed about the tragic decline of Modigliani, ravaged by drink and excess as he painted his hollow-cheeked, elongated faces with their haunting almond eyes; or about Soutine, who arrived from Lithuania in 1912, and went about dressed like a shabby old tramp, once burning his paintings in a fit of rage; or Foujita, an exotic dandy whose pictures changed hands for fabulous sums even in his lifetime. In Montparnasse artists did not only leave their work for posterity, they left their whole lives. And if this has resulted in the cliché of the artist who must either be dedicated and poverty-stricken or rich and decadent, well, there was another reality too that deserves emphasis. Rich or poor, everyone shared everything, in a communal life that reached its climax in celebratory evenings when the wine flowed freely and the girls were willing. Against this background, Chagall appeared distinctly strait-laced.

Chagall as a young man.

He devoted himself to his work, ignoring the shouts and laughter that echoed about him. Among his acquaintances he had the reputation of being something of a killjoy; afterwards none of them could remember much about him, even though they saw him every day.

The members of this closed world had one principal thing in common: all of them were strangers to Paris, many of them foreigners. Chagall's arrival in their midst was in no way remarkable. Indeed there was already a Russian contingent there, among them the sculptors Zadkine and Archipenko. Later they were to be joined by the politicians – Lenin, Trotsky and Lunacharsky.

It was this easy acceptance of new faces into a community where everyone lived and slept and worked at close quarters that made Montparnasse the international centre of bohemian life. At the Dôme or the Rotonde the painters would meet up with groups of friends or fellow-countrymen, but the true heart of the *quartier* was a little distance away from the main streets, in the direction of the Vaugirard slaughterhouses. There, in 1900, a philanthropist and sculptor called Alfred Boucher had founded a centre for penniless artists. Some one hundred and twenty studios were grouped around a wooden and brick building originally used for the World Fair, forming an artistic complex unique of its kind. It came to be called La Ruche (the 'beehive'), partly because of the distinctive polygonal shape of the central building, partly because the place was indeed a hive of activity. Chagall left the room he occupied on the Impasse du Maine and moved into a vacant studio. La Ruche hummed with life. Always there were residents coming and going, friends and visitors arriving. One of these was the poet Blaise Cendrars who, when not travelling to the ends of the earth, loved to spend his time in the cosmopolitan atmosphere of La Ruche. He became a close friend of Chagall, and wrote these lines of verse about him:

'Il dort
Il est éveillé
Tout à coup il peint
Il prend une église et peint avec une église
Il prend une vache et peint avec une vache'.
(He sleeps/He wakes/At once he paints/He chooses a church and paints a church/ He chooses a cow and paints a cow.)

It is a vivid account of the almost dreamlike directness with which Chagall approached his work, the way he would seize hold of some obvious reality and translate it into a picture. Not that his work is realistic, far from it, but it is always full of memories of things, or simply things seen – the view through a window, a studio interior, a bunch of flowers; at the root of all his lyrical transformations lies a simple and direct apprehension of the real world. In this Chagall never changed, and it is a fact worth emphasizing, given the revolution in painting that was going on all about him, notably among the Cubists.

It was during Chagall's first years in Paris, in 1910–11, that Picasso and Braque were at the height of their experiments in breaking down traditional picture perspective, thereby calling into question a convention that had been accepted practically without reservation since the Renaissance. Objects and bodies were dismembered, dissected and divided into planes that interleaved with the surface of the canvas itself. The organization of the planes was dependent on the adoption of multiple viewpoints: the single fixed viewpoint hitherto implied by the painted image was abandoned in favour of fragmentation, carried to the point sometimes where the image was barely decipherable. Objects were stripped of their traditional appearances and suggested instead by signs – notes of music, the ace of clubs, torn-off scraps of newspaper. The consequences of this radical reinterpretation of painting were enormous, and even today we have not fully assimilated the effects of the shock wave that sent its reverberations echoing through the artistic world, affecting in some degree or other every major painter of the early years of the century.

If Braque and Picasso represented Cubism in its purest form, bereft of any colour beyond a range of bistre-browns and greys, there were many other painters, such as Metzinger, Le Fauconnier, Delaunay, Léger and Gleizes, who were also characterized by the epithet coined by the critic Louis Vauxcelles as a term of abuse. Their works were all hung together in one room at the Salon des Indépendants of 1911, they had the enthusiastic support of Apollinaire, and the general impression was of a group of painters with a common aesthetic philosophy. The reality was rather different, with each pursuing his individual course, but when Chagall associated with the painters known as 'the cubists' he found himself identified with them. And it was because of their support that, in the following year, he too was able to exhibit at the annual Salon.

At the time (long before order had been imposed by the art historians), Cubism was a term used to apply to a variety of initiatives which might, broadly, be defined as anti-naturalistic in intent, rooted in an admiration for Cézanne, and attempting to represent a structure that lay beyond mere appearances. By chance, Chagall's arrival in Paris happened to coincide with a surge of creativity on many fronts. If his origins – poor, foreign and Jewish as he was – dictated that he should live and work in Montparnasse, his talents as a colourist directed him towards French painting and to Robert Delaunay in particular.

Although Delaunay was initially involved in the Cubist experiment, he soon discovered that for him it was a blind alley: the more Cubism stressed drawing and composition, even a certain classicism (on which the Section d'Or group laid particular emphasis), the more Delaunay's own art concentrated on the dynamics of colour. Lauded by Apollinaire, who called the new movement Orphism, Delaunay supplied for Chagall the solution he was already moving towards intuitively: a marriage between the modernity of Cubist pictorial space and the emotional resonance of colour.

Homage to Apollinaire, painted in 1912, was Chagall's way of signalling his gratitude to his friends – not only to the poet whose name the picture bears (it is also called *Adam and Eve*) and to the three other writers whose names are inscribed around a heart pierced by an arrow, but also to Delaunay, whose spirit the picture conjures up. Not that there is a direct debt, Chagall did not borrow from Delaunay the circular form that, in the *Simultaneous Contrasts*, was to become virtually his trademark (indeed, preliminary sketches by Chagall indicate that the shape derived from the image of a coiled snake), more it was a question of a gradual development from one drawing to the next, with increasingly geometric forms taking precedence over the overt symbolism of the theme. In that respect, certainly, the influence of Robert Delaunay is detectable, in the drive towards simplification, and in the primacy accorded to the disposition and subdivision of zones of colour.

Homage to Apollinaire serves almost as a *résumé* of the formal experiments of the period; indeed it has even been linked to the work of the Futurists, whose principal concern was the representation of movement. Looked at in this light, the wheel or clock-face on which certain numbers appear is a dynamic element indicating the passing of time, and the joined human figures become an integral part of the clock mechanism. The sheer size of the picture and its imposingly square proportions tend further to emphasize the geometric form of the couple at the expense of their humanity.

It is clear that the painting reflects in condensed form

Apollinaire and Chagall, 1910-11, gouache.

the various influences, literary and artistic, that came to bear on Chagall during his early years in Paris – the chief among these being Apollinaire, who dominated the Parisian scene. Where artistic matters were concerned, there was little that escaped him and did not receive a mention in his *Chronicles*.

Yet, given that Chagall allowed these various influences to feed into his work, the extreme stylization of the two-headed figure remains an isolated example in his iconography. In almost every other area of his work at this time the dominant theme was of a nostalgia for Russia and the Vitebsk of his childhood, imbued as it was with Hasidic Jewish culture, the place where he had left behind his sweetheart Bella, whom he had met in 1909 only shortly before he departed for Paris.

It is an extraordinary testament to the power of nostalgia that it built up in Chagall a well of creative energy, such that, there in the heart of Paris, he was able to produce an uninterrupted series of scenes of life in his home town many hundreds of miles away. These paintings fall into two main categories: those depicting peasant life, with a peasant woman and cow as protagonists (notably *To Russia, Asses and Others, The Cattle Dealer, The Angel, The Milkmaid,* etc.); and the evocation of a specifically Jewish way of life, with its familiar figures such as *The Fiddler, The Shofar,* characteristic moments (*The Pinch of Snuff, Jew at Prayer, The Sabbath, The Birth,* etc.) or occupations (*The Water Carrier, At the Barber's*), or otherwise representations of interiors and scenes conveying an atmosphere that is a distinctive blend of faith and magic. In addition, falling between these two poles, Chagall executed a series of reclining nudes and biblical characters (*Adam and Eve, Cain and Abel, Golgotha*) in which the Cubist influence is plainly apparent.

'I brought my objects from Russia and Paris gave them its light,' said Chagall. And indeed it is true that if you look back to the earlier Russian works, the use of colour is notably unadventurous. On the other hand, it is also true that Chagall's violent chromatic effects were less appreciated in Paris than they were in Berlin, thanks largely to the efforts of Herwarth Walden, a central figure in German cultural life. Famous for his encouragement of new talent, he was director of the influential review *Der Sturm*, which published the Expressionist manifestos and a defence of Kandinsky's abstraction, as well as introducing the German public to Italian Futurism and contemporary developments in French painting. In 1914, in the gallery also called Der Sturm, Walden staged Chagall's first one-man show, to a background of gunfire. Germany had a strong tradition of colourists and Romantic painters of fantastic scenes: more recently there had been Expressionists such as Jawlensky, Macke and Marc. For this reason alone Chagall was more likely to find favour here than in France – and the same was true for Robert Delaunay, regarded in Berlin as among the most influential of French painters. So it came about that it was the German collector Köhler who made the first major purchase of Chagall's work, the painting *Golgotha*, and that the exhibition of some one hundred canvases in Berlin provided the impetus for the long and brilliant career with which we are familiar.

There was nothing in Marc Chagall's background to suggest that he would become a painter, indeed it was a most unlikely course for him to follow. He was the oldest of nine children, his family lived in modest circumstances, and his father worked for a herring wholesaler. Above all, he was Jewish. For all Jews who truly honour the Holy Book, anything connected with images and representation is strictly forbidden. God is the Word, and it is sacrilege to dare to give him form; graven images belong to the world of the *goyim* (non-Jews), a curious alternative reality that is both close at hand and infinitely remote. In his memoirs, Chagall recalls how his family was incapable of coming to terms with his vocation: 'My uncle was scared to shake my hand. It was said I was a painter. What if I started drawing? It was forbidden by God. A sin.' One can only admire the far-sightedness of his mother, the rock of the family, who recognized her son's determination. Rather than putting obstacles in his way, to satisfy her own prejudices, she decided instead to take him to see a Vitebsk painter and teacher called Pen.

It would be doing a disservice to Chagall's work not to situate it in the very precise context of the life led by Jews in Russia at the turn of the century. In 1910, there were more than one and a half million Jews living in twenty-six provinces in the south and west. They were subject to many discriminatory restrictions (they could not own land or pursue certain occupations, residence permits were valid only for certain zones) and hence they lived precariously, the threat of prosecution always over their heads. In 1881, only a few years before Chagall was born, there had been an upsurge of anti-Semitic feeling and some one hundred pogroms had been carried out, leading to the first wave of emigration to Palestine. As a result of repression the Jews tended to congregate in close-knit communities, maintaining their Yiddish-based culture. In his book *L'aspect des Juifs russes*, quoted by Valentine Marcadé, B. Dinour suggests that, even in these circumstances, life had its compensations: 'It was a narrow and restricted world, affected by persecution and privation, but yet it was still a world. People were not crushed. It was even possible to be happy, there were material and spiritual sources to be tapped, a life could be made that corresponded to people's tastes and aspirations.' Apart from the small number of wealthy Jews, who were more susceptible to Russification, the vast majority of the people lived in isolation, governed by religious rules of conduct that prohibited contact with the outside world.

This, essentially, was the society into which Chagall was born and which is evoked in his pictures. But an additional factor was the influence of the Hasidic cult, to which his family belonged; that too was a crucial element in his creative inspiration.

Hasidism has its roots in nineteenth-century Eastern Europe. It is a populist pietist movement divorced from the mainstream Judaic tradition of erudition and study. The *hasid* (pious man) demonstrates his faith through his actions and thoughts rather than in his devotion to scholarly pursuits. Mysticism and, perversely, ethical struggle, lie at the heart of Hasidism. The tradition is handed down by rabbis, who have become figures of legend, and the emphasis is on prayer, singing and dancing, requiring the physical participation of the faithful. Some have claimed to see in Chagall's drawings, in his dynamic brushwork and in the facial and muscular contortions of his figures, the echo of ritual dances and swaying in time to the intoning of the psalms. But Hasidism is more than a liturgy, it is a state of mind, a way of confronting the Eternal and a way of confronting life: 'The God of the *hasidim* is engaged with you in a perpetual dialogue. He is an object of love, certainly, but also of conflict. The nature of your relationship with Him is less one of submission than of co-operation, and that co-operation may be difficult, or critical, or even tempestuous,' explains Arnold Mendel, author of *Vie quotidienne des Juifs hassidiques*. And if the *hasid* is on intimate terms with his God, it follows that he is bonded to the whole of Creation, and most nearly to the animal world. Numerous tales and legends attest to a belief in a brand of metempsychosis, in which men and animals share a common destiny that overshadows their purely temporary condition. The world that Chagall grew up in was tinged with magic, and he represented it faithfully in his paintings. The regular appearance of animals in his canvases – donkeys, cocks, goats, cows, etc. – makes sense only when it is related to a supernatural vision of the common links between all creatures, in a universe where all things are possible. 'This fundamental unreality is in tune with Hebraic iconoclasm,' suggests Franz Meyer in his account of Chagall. 'The prohibition of images was essentially intended to prevent the representation of external reality detracting from the inner reality. And Chagall, far from making his paintings subordinate to the laws of everyday reality, capable therefore of injuring the spirit, instead represents another kind of reality in which the spirit can recognize itself.'

Although drawing much of its inspiration from Hasidic culture, Chagall's work transcends its origins by espousing a form of expression that is universal: the fable. And in 1917, the time of the Russian Revolution, the fable – embodiment of popular wisdom and folk mythology – took on a new importance, indeed it acquired the status almost of a new language. The rediscovery of a rich tradition, hitherto neglected or despised, happened to coincide with Chagall's use of the form in his painting. As the Italian art historian Argan shrewdly points out: 'Almost simultaneously, Chagall with his artistic production and Proop with his scientific researches demonstrated the same thing: fable is not a tradition that is passed on passively, it is the living expression of popular creativity. And, being a historical force, it can also be a revolutionary force.' Furthermore, Chagall's iconography was deeply rooted in the language, and many of his pictures expressed in images idiomatic expressions from the Yiddish – with the result that his work, in spite of its fantastic and unconventional style, was immediately accessible to the masses, accustomed to tales colourfully told. In that respect at least, Chagall's aesthetic owed as much to Russian popular art as to Hasidic culture. And the constant reference to a broad base in popular culture provided the perfect antidote, if it were needed, to any temptation to stray into the higher reaches of the avant-garde. Set in this context, one can see

exactly what Chagall meant when he declared that Cubism was 'too realistic'. It was in fact precisely his attachment to popular imagery that made Chagall a typically Russian artist, at a time when various Western schools of painting were evolving their own independent and sophisticated iconographies. As Jean-Claude Marcadé reminds us, in his preface to the catalogue of the major exhibition of Chagall's drawings held at the Pompidou Centre in 1984: 'We should never lose sight of the fact that most of the great Russian painters who were Chagall's contemporaries (Larionov, Goncharova, Malevich, Filonov) started out from the iconographic and pictorial structure of the *lubok*'. (The *lubok* was a simple decorative image that might be anything from an embroidery motif to the pattern on a tray or snuff-box, a pastry-mould or an item of tinware.) Thus it was that an avant-garde artist like Larionov devoted himself to a sort of primitivist quest, seeking to bring out the formal richness of simple and unpretentious objects. In 1913, there were several exhibitions, such as 'The Target', which included not only works by established painters such as Chagall, Malevich and Larionov, but also children's drawings and contributions from anonymous private individuals. The great Georgian *naïf* painter Pirosmanischvili first came to public notice in this way. In general it is fair to conclude that the return to respectability of this type of marginal art was one of the by-products of the enormous aesthetic upheaval set in train in the name of modernity. In France too there was a comparable shift of taste, reflected in admiration for the Douanier Rousseau, the fashion for negro sculpture, even Gauguin's longing to escape to the South Seas. Behind it lay the same desire to find new sources, new forms, and to throw off the burden of a cultural heritage. Although, it should be said, ways of responding to these new influences varied considerably, depending on whether one happened to be painting in Moscow or Paris. In Russia 'primitive'

A rabbi at the beginning
of this century.

forms tended to be taken over virtually in their existing state – witness Larionov's pictures that are simply reproductions of graffiti.

Chagall went to Berlin for his first major exhibition, held in June 1914 at the Der Sturm gallery. In fact, unable to delay any longer, and fearing he would lose Bella's love, he was on his way back to Russia. Berlin provided a convenient stopping-place on his journey. The impression his paintings had made, and the interest they aroused, not only among the German Expressionists but also in the Parisian art world, were enough to convince him that his ultimate future lay in Western Europe, and he intended not to stay in Russia for longer than three months. Unfortunately, events were to dictate otherwise, first the outbreak of war, and then the Revolution. In the end it was not until a full eight years had elapsed that Chagall returned to France, by then a married man and a father.

When he first arrived in Vitebsk, Chagall was consumed with the need to re-experience his birthplace. In the first year he painted some sixty straightforwardly naturalistic pictures, all related to his immediate surroundings – houses, the village, portraits of brothers and sisters, mother and father, captured in familiar poses. Sitting in the room he had rented from a policeman, he painted too the view from his window (*The Birthday, Over Vitebsk*). Although his figures seem oddly unaffected by the laws of gravity, the environment is painted with a marked degree of realism, due no doubt to the fact that Chagall was now actually confronting the scene he was committing to canvas. It was as though, in Paris, distance, memory and nostalgia licensed his phantasmagoric invention, but back in Vitebsk, reality claimed its due.

It was also at this time that the painter created his imposing series of rabbis and old men, choosing his models from among the *hasidim* and dressing them in ritual costumes borrowed from his father. The paintings are often dominated by a single colour, but in each the mood is different. It is like a gallery of portraits illustrating different aspects of the Jewish soul: suffering, solitude, trust, fervour, attachment to tradition (*Jew in Yellow, Jew in Red, Jew in Green, Jew in Pink*, etc.). According to the sociologist Lucien Goldman: 'One could trace the history of Chagall's view of the Jewish world up to 1914 in the three paintings of the *Rabbi in Yellow*, the *Rabbi in Green* and *Feast Day*. Certainly the latter canvas is ironical in tone compared with the gravity of the other figures, but possibly this distancing effect is due more to the abandonment of a relatively direct realism than to any sociological factors, or to Chagall's perception of 'the Jewish world shaken and crumbling away'. More apposite seems Goldman's insight that, during this period 'Chagall simply did not notice he was living in a country at war, beyond painting a few soldiers as he recorded his impression of a street'. Certainly, we do not find Chagall serving in the trenches as an artilleryman or suffering forced marches, rather we discover him experiencing the legitimate conjugal pleasures of the newly married man.

On 25 July 1915, Bella Rosenfeld, daughter of a respected family of Jewish tradesmen who owned several jeweller's shops in the town, was married with the blessing of the synagogue to Marc Chagall. In his memoirs the painter recalls his fascination with the Rosenfeld family, who lived in elegant circumstances not far from the cathedral. The contrast with his own home could hardly have been greater: 'Their father ate grapes as mine ate onions; and the poultry we killed once a year, on the Eve of the Day of Atonement, was never off their table.' But Bella brought Chagall much more than fine food. Educated and cultured, she revealed to him whole areas of classical painting, and also shared with him her passionate love of the theatre. It was not long before visions of the blissful couple began to invade Chagall's canvases, an expression

Chagall, *The Painter before the Cathedral of Vitebsk*, 1911.

of his new-found personal happiness. His painting became sentimental, which, in view of the artistic revolution taking place elsewhere, could be seen as a retrograde step, or at least a retreat. That at any rate was the substance of Malevich's accusation against him – and it may also be the reason why his paintings are so popular today. Curiously, although the Surrealists proclaimed the subversive power of love, and made cult figures of Aragon and Elsa or Dali and Gala, they never paused to reflect on the example offered by the Chagalls.

After four years away, Chagall experienced some difficulty in taking his place again in Russian society. Obviously there was no question of resuming his student life or renewing the friendships he had made while studying under Bakst in St Petersburg. Too much had happened, and he no longer had anything in common with the brilliant set-designer of Diaghilev's Ballets Russes. The warmest welcome came from writers and intellectuals: through Bella's brother Jacov Rosenfeld, an economist dealing with problems of industrialization in a war economy, the Chagalls, living by then in Petrograd, met several of the poets made famous by the Revolution, among then Alexander Blok, Yesenin and Mayakovsky, the writer of fables Demyan Bedny, a friend of Lenin, the art critic Sirkin, Doctor Eliacheff and the Jewish collector Kagan-Chabchaj, who bought several of Chagall's paintings. In general, Chagall more than held his own with the painters then in vogue, and had several opportunities to exhibit his work, notably in 1916 with the Knave of Diamonds group, and in the following year in association with a collective of Jewish artists.

October 1917. After the 'ten days that shook the world', the Bolsheviks seized power. Chagall's circumstances were changed overnight. The new regime abolished all measures discriminating against Jews, and he found himself suddenly a full citizen with the right to travel where he pleased. No longer did he need to resort to subterfuge, as when he had arranged to be employed as a servant by his patron, the lawyer Goldberg, in order to pursue his studies in St Petersburg.

But the Revolution meant more for Chagall than political emancipation, which he shared with all the Jews in Russia. Thanks to the far-sightedness of Lunacharsky, appointed by Lenin as People's Commissar for Education and Culture, it also provided him with a unique opportunity. Anatoly Lunacharsky was the cosmopolitan intellectual *par excellence*, a larger-than-life figure who was fluent in several languages and as sympathetic to the avant-garde as he was to traditional art. In a well-documented book on the complexities of Russian culture in the post-Revolutionary period, François Champarnaud offers the following portrait of the man responsible for the arts in the newly-formed Soviet Republic: 'Humanist, aesthete and connoisseur are the words that best describe Lunacharsky. His overriding concern was to safeguard the arts, to protect Russian works of art and allow them to be seen and enjoyed by the people. In a word, to share his own love of art – which must have cost him many a sleepless night when the Revolution began.' Faced with innumerable conflicting responsibilities, obliged to strike a balance between the claims of 'proletarian culture' and the interests of the 'formalists' and 'futurists', and to reconcile these with Lenin's directives, Lunacharsky – who himself wrote several pages in eulogy of Marcel Proust – found himself in the classic position of the individual torn between his ideals and the requirements of political expediency. Although he was toppled from power on Lenin's death, it was under his influence that the USSR enjoyed its most fertile period of artistic and cultural activity. Lunacharsky had met Chagall in Paris, in those heady days in Montparnasse. Recognizing his talent, and also his devotion to Vitebsk, in late 1918 he offered him the position of director – or commissar, as it was then called – of the School of Fine Arts in his native town. Chagall's responsibilities were wide-ranging. Among his tasks was 'to organize the art schools, museums, exhibitions, conferences and all other artistic activities in the town and region of Vitebsk', with, in addition, a requirement to oversee the running of the theatres. It was in this context that Chagall made his preparations for the first anniversary of the Revolution, to be celebrated in Vitebsk with as much brilliance and spendour as if it were Moscow or Petrograd.

The Soviet festivities celebrating the Revolution were one of the great occasions in the history of twentieth-century art. The Utopian and subversive themes of the avant-garde were, for once, in total accord with a popular desire for a re-shaping of society. The result was a fusion of interests, an immense surge of creativity that had hitherto been confined to the artistic sphere. It is true that this extraordinary conjunction of the interests of art and society existed for two or three years at the most, but while it lasted extraordinary things were achieved. Traditional boundaries were broken down, so that theatrical performance overlapped with spontaneous participation, Futurist calligraphy with political sloganizing, stage design with civic planning. Sometimes the results were spectacular. 'The united participation of the various art forms, against the background of the old town, was aimed at creating a sort of "city of the future", not of course in the sense of an actual architectural construction, but rather as a design for new feelings and ideology, expressed through art,' explains the Soviet historian Anatoly Strigalev. The transformation of Vitebsk was verging on the miraculous: 'Some three hundred and fifty transparencies were suspended about the town. Seven triumphal arches had been erected on the main squares, together with vast grandstands for the people. Countless

flags fluttered in the streets, everywhere was decorated with leafy garlands, and at night the whole place was illuminated,' writes Meyer, who detects behind the extravaganza the 'fantastic imagination of Chagall'. Even artists such as Malevich and Lissitzky contributed to the Vitebsk celebrations with abstract and geometric decorations that represented the avant-garde at its most extreme. Only the mood of a society in ferment, still intoxicated by its recent emancipation, can begin to explain the spirit of freedom that was abroad in the streets, and which made possible acts that even today would be regarded as daring. 'People had even decked the trains and streets with non-figurative paintings,' Rippelino tells us in his study of *Maïakowsky et le théâtre russe*. 'Huge decorative panels concealed the crumbling façades of the old buildings. As they strolled about, the Russian people had the opportunity to admire vast décors by Chagall, Alexandra Exter, Sterenberg and Altman. Vitebsk was translated into a fairyland of modern painting: the tramways and shop windows and houses were decked with brilliant colour.'

In fulfilling his official functions, Chagall succeeded in making Vitebsk one of the leading artistic centres, with the School of Fine Arts giving the lead. The Academy laid stress on professional activity: in its 'community studios', pupils worked side by side with independent artists already successful in their own right; the products of the studios – posters, displays, murals or theatre-sets – were designed to serve the needs of the wider community. In Chagall, the Academy had a conscientious director who took his administrative responsibilities seriously. He was assiduous in seeking out sources of finance, and concerned to enhance the School's reputation by employing only the best teachers. The studio for graphic arts and architecture was headed by El Lissitzky, an indefatigable propagandist in the cause of Soviet revolutionary art; he was a frequent visitor to Germany, where he moved in

Chagall teaching in the
Malakhovska War Orphan Colony
near Moscow in 1921.

Chagall and the committee members of the Vitebsk Academy in 1919.

Dadaist circles, and regarded it as his mission to travel throughout Europe bringing news of the latest developments on the artistic front, and attempting to unite opposing philosophies. Not with unmixed success, however, as events were soon to prove. Nevertheless, there are many positive achievements to Lissitzky's name: he collaborated with Chagall on a project of illustrating Jewish books, taking his inspiration largely from folk art, and later worked within the orbit of Malevich's Suprematism, attempting the impossible task of reconciling it with its arch-enemy, Constructivism. Although this is not the moment to enter into the rights and wrongs of a bitter dispute, in which Chagall himself refused to become embroiled, it is relevant to note that, while in Vitebsk, Lissitzky created his famous *Story of Two Squares*, which caused a small revolution in the aesthetics of typography. It was, after all, Lissitzky who brought about Chagall's abrupt departure from Vitebsk, in 1920. Lissitzky had asked Chagall to invite to the Academy the charismatic Malevich, whom he greatly admired. In so doing he failed to take into account the obvious incompatibility of temperament and artistic philosophy that divided the two men. Malevich was a strong personality with many disciples; he saw his Suprematist movement invading every sphere of life and serving as the cornerstone for all artistic development in the future. While Chagall was away in Moscow, trying to obtain 'bread, paint and money', Malevich and his group took over the Academy and renamed it the Suprematist Academy – as a large banner outside proclaimed. When Chagall returned, he found himself faced with a show of strength, and chose to resign. Although a majority of the pupils begged him to change his mind, he determined to move to Moscow. Apparently he had no great stomach for a fight. Whether this was because he was temperamentally disinclined to political in-fighting, or because Bella influenced him, or even be-

cause he feared he would not have the backing of the authorities, we shall probably never know. What is clear – although it is not widely appreciated – is that he actively supported the new cultural regime and was strenuously opposed to the Suprematist's leader, who appears in this tale in a less than flattering light.

In spite of these setbacks, Chagall was regarded as a painter whose work expressed the new spirit abroad in Russia. In 1919, the first Official Exhibition of Revolutionary Art was held in the fabulous surroundings of the old Winter Palace in Petrograd – scene of a famous insurrection, now renamed the Palace of the Arts. Intended as a grand survey of artistic activity, the exhibition included works by 359 artists. Chagall's 15 large canvases, far from being relegated to obscurity, were hung in pride of place in the first two rooms. The position of honour accorded him, and the fact that he was extravagantly praised by the critics and had half a dozen canvases purchased by the state, are all indications of the esteem in which Chagall was held among 'revolutionary' artists. And indeed, before the grisly spectacle began of the Revolution 'devouring its children', there was no obligation to espouse a political philosophy or toe the party line. Chagall was able to say, with equanimity: 'My knowledge of Marxism was limited to an awareness that Marx was a Jew and had a long beard.' (*My Life*).

When he moved to Moscow in 1920, Chagall nevertheless kept his distance from the wilder manifestations of *agitprop*, which regarded art and politics as indissolubly linked. Leaving social ferment to others, he turned his attention to the most imaginative of fictional forms, the theatre.

In the past Chagall had showed no particular interest in the stage, and it was Bella – who when at school in Moscow had attended courses given by the Realist director Stanislavsky – who introduced her husband to its fascinations.

Chagall, *Study,* 1918.

In pre-Revolutionary Russia, theatrical style was the subject of impassioned debate; the stage was the obvious arena in which artists could experiment with the creation of a living art that intervened directly in space and was not destined to end its days in a dusty museum. Meyerhold, implacably opposed to the Naturalist tendencies of his former teacher Stanislavsky, staged performances of an avant-garde character, the sets designed by Constructivist or Suprematist painters. 'Meyerhold, red scarf about his neck, with the profile of an Emperor in exile, is the main-stay of the theatrical revolution,' said Chagall, adding, 'I love him, only him out of all of them. I am only sorry I never worked with him.' One can well believe it: they would have had much in common, including a fierce dislike of Naturalism. Chagall's approach to painting was ideally suited to theatre design – as one can see, with hindsight, from his sets for *Aleko* and his decoration of the ceiling of the Paris Opéra.

Apart from the strategic position occupied by the theatre in Russian cultural life (rather different from the situation in France, where the theatre has always been

Chagall, *Man with Lamp*, 1921.

regarded primarily as a literary medium), there was an-other and more immediate reason why Chagall was drawn to the stage, and that was connected with the revival of Jewish literature and arts. The basis of this renaissance was the official recognition of the Yiddish tongue, no longer regarded as a vulgar corruption but as a full language in its own right, with a body of authors to its name. The most popular of these was Sholem Aleichem, who achieved an international reputation. He specialized in writing 'miniatures', colourful monologues related by the inhabitants of a typical Jewish community, or *shtetl*; in pungent language, the characters expressed their joys and sorrows – joys and sorrows such as Aleichem himself had experienced. He had started out in life with nothing, but married into a wealthy family and acquired a modest

Chagall, *Movement,* 1921.

Chagall, *Abduction,* 1920.

fortune, which he promptly frittered away with bad management and acts of misplaced generosity. He lived in Odessa and then Kiev, until he was driven out by the pogrom of 1905, and died in New York in 1916. Sholem Aleichem was the very incarnation of Hasidic culture – one of whose precepts was that Yiddish should be preferred to Hebrew for prayer because 'when you are not familiar with a language, the heart does not follow the words you utter'. So at least said Rabbi Nahman of Braslav, a legendary figure aptly described by Elie Wiesel as representing 'the celebration of the word, the apotheosis of the winged legend, inspired and intoxicating'. The fact that Hasidism was essentially a popular movement, with a deep-rooted culture of its own, explains why it was favourably regarded by the Bolshevik state. Although not

remotely secular in intention, books, newspapers, schools and theatres were all encouraged; Yiddish became an official language of the Soviet Union and was taught in the universities until 1948.

It was in this changed context that, in 1920, the modest Jewish theatre company in Petrograd, founded by a group of amateurs, was officially designated a state theatre and transferred to a 90-seat auditorium in Moscow. Three of Aleichem's monologues were to open the season, *The Agents, The Lie* and *Mazeltov.* Chagall was the obvious choice to design the sets. His sketches, reassembled for the major retrospective of drawings held at the Pompidou Centre in 1984, reveal an unexpectedly abbreviated style: concrete elements are suggested merely by signs, so that a train, for example, is represented by a luggage-rack, and the rails by the simple arc of a circle (*The Agents*). Probably there is an unconscious debt to Suprematism in this severe economy of means and minimalist reduction of the forms, which allow each colour to take on the significance of a symbol.

But Chagall's greatest contribution to Jewish art was

in the form of the murals he created for the theatre building itself (sadly, now kept hidden from the public gaze by the Soviet authorities). Commissioned by the artistic director Granowsky, at the suggestion of Effross, these decorations cover the three walls of the auditorium, and they are without question the best illustration we have of the ritual gestures and postures of the cult of Hasidism. It is known that the great actor Michoëls referred to them, and used Chagall's rhythmic arabesques as the model for his own portrayals of religious fervour.

Among art historians a fierce debate continues to rage (not entirely unaffected by political prejudices) as to the precise causes and timing of the reaction against avant-garde art in the Soviet Union, which ushered in the most repressive cultural counter-revolution known to history. Given the ambiguous stance adopted by the artists themselves, the introduction of the NEP (New Economic Policy), the death of Lenin and subsequent rise and triumph of Stalinism, it becomes almost impossible to make a judgment. Suffice it to say that they were all contributory factors to the wholesale artistic repression that followed, and that when Chagall decided to leave the Soviet Union in 1922, he was merely anticipating by two or three years the fall from grace that inevitably awaited him; exile was most certainly the wiser course.

As we have seen, it was in Germany, the home of Expressionism, that Chagall's work found particular favour, above all among the younger artists and writers; individuals as different as Kurt Schwitters and Max Ernst have recorded their amazement on first seeing his paintings. There was every reason why Chagall should think of returning there, especially as many of his canvases had remained in Berlin after Walden's exhibition. But much had changed since his first visit eight years previously. Russia and Germany had fought on opposite sides in the War. A Revolution had taken place. It was widely assumed in Berlin that Russia was in a state of total devastation, and that Chagall had probably perished in the turmoil. Indeed, a man who has never been identified took advantage of the general confusion and breakdown of communications to pass himself off as Chagall. Many people knew the name but had no idea what the painter looked like, so that the enterprising trickster succeeded in gaining access to some of the best houses in Berlin. Meyer, who relates the anecdote, does not offer any further details, but it seems likely that such impostures were common. When the real Chagall made his appearance, it was rather like a ghost returning from the dead, and there were stormy scenes with Walden, who had sold off the canvases left at the gallery. Inevitably there were arguments about money, unresolved even by a court case. A sort of Alice in Wonderland situation prevailed in the German economy, and inflation had reached staggering proportions. The citizens of the country felt reality slipping away from under them, as though in a nightmare. Klaus Mann explains: 'We experienced the total collapse of the one value in which a godless age truly put its faith: money. Money simply evaporated away and disappeared into astronomical figures. Seven and a half million marks to the dollar. American tourists bought Baroque furniture for the equivalent of a mouthful of bread. A genuine Dürer was worth two bottles of whisky … The mark was waltzing downhill, why shouldn't we join the dance.' Berlin, with its population of disinherited people, seemed to be living through the last act of the imperial drama, a grotesque suicidal frenzy reflected with trenchant irony in the famous cabarets of the day. 'In the apartments by the Bayrische Platz there were almost as many samovars and Theosophist or Tolstoyan countesses as there used to be in Russia,' was Chagall's dry comment. 'In the Russian restaurants on the Motzstrasse there were more Russian generals and colonels, working now as cooks and bottle-

Chagall preparing the sketch for
Introduction to the Jewish Theatre.

Chagall and his family in 1923-4 in the studio on the Avenue d'Orléans in Paris.

washers, than you would find in a Czarist garrison town. As for me, I have never in my life seen so many miracle-working rabbis as in Berlin in 1922.' Such scenes could hardly pass unnoticed by the former Expressionists: in vivid sketches, George Grosz, Otto Dix and Max Beckmann satirized the troubled creatures who haunted Berlin society, the drug dealers, the prostitutes, the pimps. But Chagall, busy learning new techniques of engraving and lithography, kept his eyes firmly fixed on Vitebsk and his memories of childhood.

Chagall stayed in Germany for a full year, dividing his time between Berlin and Kaunas, in the Black Forest. He had travelled on a passport supplied by Lunacharsky and arranged for his canvases to be sent on by diplomatic bag – which was finally achieved with the help of the Lithuanian ambassador, none other than the eminent art historian Jürgis Baltrusaïtis, author of marvellous works on anamorphism, mirrors and optical devices. Bella had suffered a fall during the rehearsal of a play and had been unable to accompany her husband. She and her young daughter joined him some months later, and the family stayed for a while in Kaunas before travelling together to Paris.

Leaving Russia behind them, the Chagalls embarked on a new life. Paris was the ultimate destination of a journey begun some ten years previously, prolonged by circumstances beyond their power to predict. Not unreasonably, what they hoped for now was a little peace and stability in their lives. This Paris supplied them with in ample measure, along with an increasing prosperity (reflected in their several moves from the Avenue d'Orléans to the smart sixteenth *arrondissement*) and a circle of good and loyal friends. Many of these were writers: Jean Paulhan, René Schwob, Max Jacob, Supervielle, Eluard and, of course, Cendrars. It was through his old friend of Montparnasse days that Chagall met the influential dealer Ambroise Vollard, a phenomenal man who somehow seemed to have the knack of anticipating the rest in buying up Cézanne or Matisse, Maillol or Picasso, or almost any other promising artist you might care to name.

The encounter with Vollard was particularly stimulating for Chagall as it persuaded him to venture into a new area of work: book illustration. As well as being a dealer, Vollard was a publisher of note; he was particularly keen to work with Chagall and therefore shrewdly allowed him to make his own choice of text. Chagall, being familiar with the works of Gogol through set-designs for his plays, put forward a proposal to illustrate *Dead Souls*.

The result was to be a masterpiece of humour and sensitivity, the poetry of the text and the fantasy of the images vying with each other in defying the logic of the real world. To Jean-Claude Marcadé, the symbiotic relationship that was established between Gogol and Chagall was proof of the latter's essentially Russian character, which went way beyond his Hasidic origins, and enabled him to get to the roots of the language itself. 'Gogol's powerfully plastic language produces an extraordinarily varied scheme of formal devices, drawn from metamorphoses of reality, from the realm of dreams and nightmares and from hyperbole – a scheme to which Chagall could not have responded unless he experienced a natural affinity with it,' he suggests, not dissenting substantially from Nabokov's description of Gogol's work, in his penetrating and lucid study, as 'a prodigy of language, not of ideas'. It is, no doubt, significant to recall that Chagall had previously shown an interest in language in his paintings based on Yiddish idiom. It is also relevant to note that, in the process of illustrating a literary text, Chagall was forced to move away from his usual subject-matter without however changing his characteristic handling. Here the usual problems in distinguishing style from content do not apply. The engraved plates for *Dead Souls* are of considerable interest, for they show a man in full possession of his talents, capable of being true to himself within guidelines established by another creative mind. Paradoxically, it is often true that an artist reveals himself most clearly in a minor genre such as engraving rather than in the mainstream of his painting. In this respect the example of Chagall – primarily regarded as a colourist – is particularly instructive.

The hidden relationship between art and language in Chagall's work did not escape the notice of André Breton, a specialist in such matters. In his usual dogmatic fashion, the 'pope' of Surrealism proclaimed that 'only with him did metaphor make its triumphal entry onto the scene of modern art'. But if we accept that one of the prime concerns of the modern movement was to find ways of eliminating the narrative content of the image, if not the image itself, then it becomes clear that Chagall's *oeuvre* must occupy a somewhat ambivalent position within that movement. Chagall's conception of a pictorial space liberated from the conventions of Realism (the observation of scale and colour values), its poetic content founded in free associations of fantasy and reality, would tend to place him fairly and squarely on the side of modernity. As an artist, he was above all concerned to find new ways of expressing feeling. But his work also contains a 'message', a simple expression of a universal theme – the rehabilitation of Jewish culture, evocation of the homeland, the happiness of shared love – and in that it is in direct contradiction to the avant-garde goal of eradicating meaning from the image. Even within the marginal ranks of artists, Chagall stood alone. And he was more than happy to do so, refusing to accept that the Cubists and Suprematists and Constructivists were innovators at all. In fact he accused them of Realism, and in many ways he was right. To Chagall the creation of a picture meant the construction of a mental space, inhabited by the subjective feelings of the artist; that was why he kept return-

ing to the same themes and was almost obsessional in using certain figures over and over again – the couple, flowers, the village, animals. In other words, a picture by Chagall would use a limited range of subjects to express a poetic vision, in comparison with which anything else, be it a Suprematist triangle or a Cubist head, was Realism pure and simple. If poets like Cendrars, Aragon and Eluard were capable of appreciating Chagall's work, it was because it dealt, in its own terms, with concepts and feelings with which they were familiar. In that sense Breton was absolutely right to see metaphor in Chagall's painting. One need only take the example of the couple floating in the air, which is the crystallization of feeling so intense that language itself can only express it in terms of images of flight and weightlessness.

It would be hard to conceive of poetry, or poetic art, that ignored the subject of love. But it has to be remembered that in the artistic revolution of the early years of the century all the established values were being questioned. In France in particular, painting had little time for the finer feelings and concentrated instead on human frailty, bodily grace and sensuality, as immortalized by Matisse or Gauguin. In this emotional desert there was however one other painter who allowed subjective feeling to dictate the nature of the world he painted, and that was Giorgio de Chirico. Although in many ways Chagall's opposite, he shared with him a desire to restore to the image its powers of suggestion. On the face of it there could be nothing more different from the Vitebsk painter's rabbis and cows than the echoing arcades and empty squares favoured by the inventor of metaphysical painting. What the two artists had in common, however, was a rejection of the prevailing aesthetic of the years 1910–25. This was pointed out by Paul Fierens in an article published in the review *L'Amour de l'Art*, in 1925: 'Giorgio de Chirico is, with Chagall, one

Chagall, illustration for Gogol's *Dead Souls*, published in 1949.

of the rare modern artists not to be frightened of the imagination.' A point had been reached where it was, literally, eccentric to give vent to feelings of melancholy or love. That is why Apollinaire too, even as early as 1914, instinctively compared the two painters (they were exact contemporaries, and members of his own artistic circle), concluding that 'Chirico was more classical than Chagall'. And in 1957, André Breton, in an article entitled *L'Art magique*, simply took it as read that Chirico, Chagall and Marcel Duchamp were all working in the same area.

The opinion of Breton, author of the Surrealist manifesto, is very much to the point. When Chagall returned to Paris the ascendant literary and artistic movement, the topic of conversation in all the cafés, was Surrealism. Chagall was given a respectful reception by the leaders of the group but, even though his work was a celebration of an imaginary world, and therefore very close in spirit to the territory they claimed as their own, he never became part of the movement, or even, like Chirico, regarded it with sympathy. In some ways it is hard to see why, since the Surrealist insistence on an irrational, dreamlike representation of the world must have had much to recommend it to the painter of *The Reclining Poet* and *The Dream*. But, once again, Chagall showed himself reluctant to identify himself with a theory – and one knows how intransigent Breton could be on matters of doctrine. There was also the question of the Jewishness of Chagall's work. Even though by its very existence it flouted religious orthodoxy, to the Surrealists it suggested a guilty attachment to beliefs quite incompatible with free-thinking.

As soon as he was back in the French capital, Chagall was eager to recover the canvases he had left behind in his studio at La Ruche. When he departed for Russia he had simply secured the door with a piece of wire, and, of course, the inevitable had happened. Everything had disappeared. His immediate priority was therefore to recreate the body of reference works he felt he needed in order to advance. Working either from memory, or using photographs, he began the task of repainting some of the canvases that had either disappeared or been abandoned in Russia, and also made copies of certain works still in his possession. It is to his desire to retrace the landmarks of a career disrupted by travelling that we owe the existence of the 1924 versions of *The Pinch of Snuff, The Birthday, Jew in Black and White, Above the Town* and *Over Vitebsk*. This brief tour of the past – which took in a smaller version of *Introduction to the Jewish Theatre* called *The Acrobats* (later cut by the artist into two sections, entitled *The Circus* and *The Harlequins*) – was also a kind of farewell, a triumphant lap of honour. For as Chagall's life began to change, and he experienced both financial and emotional security, so too his painting underwent a transformation. His canvases were flooded with the rich colours of the natural world and the subtle variations of light; his iconography expanded to express contentment and relish in the pleasures and beauties of life. The profound melancholy that had cast a shade over his first stay in Paris was dissipated in delight at the French countryside, discovered on expeditions with his family. A weekend at L'Isle-Adam with the Delaunays, a trip to the Normandy coast in April, then to the Ile de Bréhat in Brittany . . . The Chagalls made these excursions a regular feature of their life. And as they travelled, so Chagall's painting, like a sensitized plate, recorded the changes in atmosphere; his colours became more airy and diffuse, his handling more broken. His canvases were filled with rustic scenes, views of the countryside seen from a window, bunches of flowers. Also farmyard scenes, which provided the opportunity to paint animals, man's friends and allies – a theme that was to be brought to a pitch of perfection in a series of gouaches illustrating the *Fables* of La Fontaine, commissioned once again by Vollard. The thirty or so works were executed while Chagall was staying near Lac Chambon in the Auvergne, and the violence of the colour and imaginative brushwork – impasto, drips and sprays – were directly inspired by the dramatic effects of the light in these surroundings of natural beauty.

Chagall's activity was unremitting. After the *Fables*, he started work on a series on the theme of the circus, once again for Vollard. The dealer had his own box at the Cirque d'Hiver, and Chagall often went with him to performances. The circus was a subject perfectly suited to Chagall's interest in weightlessness, balance and contortion, and he produced a number of major oils on these themes. His favourite subjects were the equestriennes and bareback riders and the acrobats. Then there were the canvases of lovers floating in the air, against a background of the Eiffel Tower and the roofs of Paris, the numerous bouquets of flowers, in short, a dazzling display of talent on all fronts. In the course of his travels, Chagall also discovered the Côte d'Azur, loved by so many painters for the quality of the southern light. (Chagall was to prove no exception, moving to live there permanently in 1950.) With Delaunay he toured in south-west France, visiting the writer Joseph Delteil in Limoux, and making a pilgrimage to Collioure in honour of Maillol. And when the Chagalls encountered the snowy landscapes of the Pyrenees and the Alps, memories of Russia rose to the surface, and the paintings took on a hue of milky whiteness.

In the early thirties, encouraged once again by Vollard, Chagall embarked on the vast project of illustrating the Bible. Although it was a world familiar to him since childhood, when the prophets seemed rather like distant cousins who might arrive on a visit at any moment, it was nevertheless a daunting task. Engraving is a highly complex and skilled technique, demanding great concentration and single-mindedness from the artist. The pace of the work was very slow, and the illustrations were to occupy Chagall until after the War; in the event, the 105 plates were not published until 1957, by which time Vollard had died and the project had been taken over by Tériade. Before starting work, Chagall had determined to visit the Holy Land. In 1931, with his wife Bella and daughter Ida accompanying him, he embarked ship for Alexandria. Together they visited Cairo and the Pyramids (at a time when the monuments of Upper Egypt attracted only the professional archaeologists), and then moved on to Palestine. For Chagall the country was a revelation. Actually to see for himself the holy places, surrounded by slopes covered with orange groves, in the golden light and silence of the nearby desert, was – as other travellers of the time have attested – an experience of indelible significance and beauty.

Chagall painted a number of pictures in Palestine and, as had happened once before when he returned to Vitebsk, the overwhelming presence of the landscape brought out in him a latent strand of Realism. He returned from Jerusalem with an astonishing version of *The Wailing Wall*, each block of stone from Solomon's Temple rendered with a dramatic potency that was transmitted intact to the subsequent engravings. It was as though something of his Hasidic iconoclasm had been dissipated.

Between 1932 and 1937, the Chagalls travelled extensively in Europe. In Holland they went to see the Rembrandts (whose influence is detectable in certain engravings and in the later *Biblical Message*), and they toured Spain with Supervielle and Michaux. In the following year they went to Poland, in response to an invitation to attend the opening ceremony of the Jewish Institute in Vilna. Among the Polish Jews, whose situation was worsening daily, Chagall found himself for the first time in many years in a world geographically and emotionally close to Vitebsk, now barred to him for ever. Instinctively

Chagall at work on the portrait *Bella in Green* in 1934.

he felt the need to paint scenes of the interiors of synagogues, as though he sensed the impending Holocaust that was to devastate his people and threaten the survival of their way of life. Other of his major compositions of the late thirties echo to the sounds of jackboots and gunfire then beginning to be heard throughout Europe. In *White Crucifixion* and *Revolution* a new protagonist appeared: the people.

Yet such works remain the exception, even in those politically troubled times. Right up to the moment of his enforced departure for the United States, the beginning of a second period of exile (for Chagall had acquired French citizenship in 1937), he continued to paint subjects drawn from his private mythology (*The Cellist, Midsummer Night's Dream, Bride and Groom of the Eiffel Tower*) or explorations of the unconscious, such as *Time is a River without Banks*, which depicts a curious flying machine made up of a clock attached to a winged fish, flying through space like an indecipherable enigma.

In times of trouble, art can provide a refuge, and Chagall threw himself into his work with a single-minded passion that is unique in this century. The sheer scale of his output demonstrated his unshakeable belief in life and the powers of creativity. But his bright colours were of little avail against the brown-shirted menace that was creeping over Europe. Once again Chagall was to be forced into exile, threatened this time by a barbarism of a new order, in comparison with which even the pogroms of the past paled. Yet he hesitated to the last, lingering on in Gordes, in Provence, deaf to the urgent pleadings of his friends and ignoring an officially inspired invitation from the Museum of Modern Art in New York. It was not until the first anti-Jewish measures were introduced that he woke up to the danger. On 7 May, with his wife and child, he left Marseille for the New World. Two months later he was miraculously reunited with the 1,500

kilos of luggage he had managed to ship out before he left. It contained all his work.

In the nineteen-forties, New York was like the Babylon of the modern age. Fleeing the Nazi threat, the foremost intellectuals of Europe arrived there by the boatload. Many were profoundly disorientated by the experience of being transplanted suddenly to a cosmopolitan world, far removed from their familiar surroundings, and it was inevitable that there was much extravagant behaviour. 'It is difficult to convey the atmosphere of New York in the early forties, with its heterogeneous society of artistic refugees, among them Dali, ruling the roost, closely rivalled by Pavel Tchelichev and Eugène Berman, who designed sets and costumes for the Ballets Russes,' writes Robert Lebel, from the vantage-point of an eye-witness. 'Amid this throng, the appearance of international stars like Chagall, Léger, Mondrian, and the Surrealists, Matta, Tanguy, Max Ernst, Breton and Masson, to name them in order of arrival, went at first unnoticed.' Chagall had more experience than most at adapting to new conditions and, even though he spoke not a word of English, rapidly acquired a circle of friends and gained an entrée to the gallery run by Pierre Matisse. His immediate circumstances were tolerable, but his paintings reveal a preoccupation with suffering, expressed in images of Christ on the Cross, such as *Crucifixion in Yellow, The Martyr* and *Obsession*. Filled with Judaic references and peopled with the artist's familiar creatures, these lie outside the mainstream of Christian iconology. It is clear that the image presented of Christ's agony has a more than purely religious significance, it is also the emblem of the suffering of a whole people. There is just one sign of Chagall's irrepressible love of life, and that is the introduction into his bestiary of a new and lusty presence, that of the cock.

Through his links with the Russian colony in New York, Chagall met Igor Stravinsky, and also renewed an

New York in 1942, front row from left to right: Matta Echaurren, Ossip Zadkine, Yves Tanguy, Max Ernst, Marc Chagall, Fernand Léger; back row from left to right: André Breton, Piet Mondrian, André Masson, Amédée Ozenfant, Jacques Lipchitz, Pavel Tchelitchew, Kurt Seligmann, Eugene Berman.

old acquaintance with Léonid Massine, the celebrated choreographer of the Ballets Russes. Both asked him to work on sets for forthcoming productions. For Massine, Chagall designed the sets and backcloths for *Aleko*, a one-act ballet based on Pushkin's *The Gypsies*, with music by Tchaikovsky. It was his first opportunity since *Introduction to the Jewish Theatre* to work on a monumental scale, and it proved he was as much at home with the broad panorama of stage design as he was with the minutiae of engraving. Indeed, his colour actually gained in intensity and nuance, as the opening curtain shows: the expanse of blue structures space by subtle gradations of tone, quite independent of the figurative motifs. Chagall's pictorial space was, in general, becoming increasingly dominated by colour, and there is a discernible progression from *Aleko*, through his designs for *The Firebird*, to the ceiling of the Paris Opéra, painted in 1964. By the time of the latter work, the coloured background has become an independent space, on which the drawn figures are superimposed – rather in the way that music serves as the indispensable basis without which singing or ballet cannot exist. *Aleko* was very much a Russian collaboration – not only was it directed by Léonid Massine, but the original author, the composer and the designer were also Russian. The world première was held in Mexico on 10 September 1942, and the production moved to New York on 6 October, with resounding success. Chagall's reputation on the American continent was assured.

With his sets for Stravinsky's ballet *The Firebird*, executed in 1942, Chagall surpassed even the expectations aroused by *Aleko*. The shimmering colour of the 'oriental' costumes reminded audiences of the magnificent creations devised by Léon Bakst for Diaghilev, but they above all responded to the brilliance with which the audacities of the new music were matched by the modernity of the sets. Once again, the occasion was a triumph.

For Chagall, his time in America was an opportunity to look beyond easel-painting to the challenge offered by stage design. A major retrospective of his work toured from New York to Chicago, further enhancing his reputation. But amid professional success came personal tragedy: his wife Bella was taken ill and died in September 1944.

The War over, Chagall determined to return to France. As though to welcome him, a major exhibition of his work was held in the autumn of 1947 at the Musée d'Art Moderne. This was followed by other exhibitions all over Europe: at the Stedelijk Museum, Amsterdam; the Tate Gallery in London; the Kunsthaus in Zurich; the Kunsthalle in Bern; the Venice Biennale. Chagall was recognized as one of the great painters of the twentieth century, an artist capable of working on the grand scale. Commissions poured in, and, at the age of sixty, he found himself launched on a new international career. Thanks to his exceptional energy he was able to respond to its demands, remaining active as a painter until the age of ninety-seven.

Rather than going back to live in Paris, Chagall chose to make his permanent home in a villa called Les Collines, in Vence. Like Picasso, Matisse and Bonnard before him, he was drawn there by the Mediterranean light and the sweetness of life in Provence. In those post-war years, the South of France was a focal point of artistic activity, and a local dealer called Aimé Maeght had connections with most of the great painters of the day. Chagall became one of the principal exhibitors at his gallery.

New influences led Chagall to diversify his forms. An interest in ceramics introduced him to the complexities of volume. Not far away were the famous potteries of Vallauris, frequented by Picasso, a centre for the production of vases, plates and mural decorations. Chagall began to experiment with sculpture, producing a number of figurines and roughly hewn statues; in marble, stone

or tufa, his heads of Christ, Moses and David have something of the archaic quality of Gauguin's sculptures in wood, or of Roman capitals. His talents as a ceramicist found a new outlet through an extraordinary and visionary man called Father Couturier, who regarded it as his mission in life to bring about a union between modern art and Christianity; the Church of Notre-Dame on the Plateau d'Assy was to stand as the living monument to that collaboration. Inspired as much by religious as artistic ideals, he succeeded against all the odds in enlisting the co-operation of such figures as Bonnard, Braque, Léger, Matisse, Rouault, Miró, Lurçat, Lipchitz and Laurens, overcoming the inevitable problems of bringing together artists so very different, and dealing with the very real difficulties of financing such a project. Father Couturier might have had the art of Marc Chagall specifically in mind when he declared his belief that 'in every artist the purest and most irreplaceable sources of inspiration spring from a particular inner realm in which reason and personal will cease to be operative, namely the hidden and enduring realm of childhood. That is the wonderland that the great artists keep with them all their lives as the most pure and precious part of themselves'.

The task allotted to Chagall was the decoration of the baptismal chapel; his response was in the form of a ceramic mural of Moses parting the waters of the Red Sea, juxtaposed with two high reliefs, their combined effect such as to make the confined space glow with wonderful modulations of light and colour. The church as a whole is a testament to the vision of a Dominican father whose belief in modern art matched his religious faith. It remains today the finest example of the blossoming of the craft movement (stained glass, ceramics, mosaic-work and tapestry) that occurred in the nineteen-fifties. For Chagall the experience was of particular significance, and he became increasingly interested in the integration of coloured surfaces with architecture. The natural brilliance of his palette found a new expression in stained glass, the perfect meeting-point of colour and luminosity. In 1952, after studying at length the windows of Chartres Cathedral, he began to experiment with this form of representation which, through the ages, has used coloured light to represent the visible yet insubstantial presence of spirituality. For the cathedrals of Metz and Rheims, the synagogue of the Hadassah Clinic in Jerusalem, and in various projects in the United States, he produced stained-glass

Chagall in Vence in 1958.

Chagall preparing the sketch
for the ceiling of the Opéra,
Vence, 1963.

Chagall touching up the Opéra ceiling.

windows that are the apotheosis of colour. They go to the very heart of Chagall's artistic vision: as colour spreads over monumental surfaces, dematerialized by the transparency of the glass, it undergoes a transmutation and becomes elemental, transformed into an energy that sets space alight. It is as though something is released that in the paintings can be no more than a latent possibility, the colours trapped within the confines of their pigments.

Indeed, colour is the key to understanding Chagall's development as an artist. Over the years it took on an increasing importance in his work, not only becoming bolder and brighter, but 'laying a growing role in structuring the composition. When he first arrived in France, Chagall declared that Paris gave his painting light; in all probability a similar illumination took place when he went to live in Provence on his return from America. Life in the Mediterranean region, and his second marriage, in 1952, to Valentine (Vava) Brodsky, followed by a memorable trip to Greece, all combined to induce in him a new serenity and contemplativeness, rooted in a sensual appreciation of colour. The early fifties produced a cycle of paintings based on Paris (*The Banks of the Seine, Quai de Bercy, The Carrousel of the Louvre*, and others), taking in most of the capital's great monuments. Yet the intention was less to offer a panorama of tourists' Paris than to explore ways of juxtaposing colour, henceforth to be laid out in zones; thus these paintings can be read in two ways at once, as chromatic schemes verging on abstraction, or as anecdotal figurations.

With disarming ease, the painter made the transition from the scale of the traditional canvas to vast mural commissions; it is as though his winged creatures could not wait to regain their natural habitat, attaching themselves to the heights of a ceiling or clinging to a wall. The enchanted world summoned up in Chagall's painting was, as we have already pointed out, the perfect complement to the bustle and brilliance of the theatrical auditorium. Malraux asked him to decorate the ceiling of the Paris Opéra in 1964, and this was followed by commissions for the foyer of the principal theatre in Frankfurt and from the Metropolitan Opera, New York (1965).

In the face of such prodigality one might be tempted to believe Chagall was under some compulsion to be always in the public eye – his works are present in every corner of the world, mosaics and tapestries (even in the Knesset, the Israeli parliament building), stained-glass windows and wall-paintings, decorating public buildings and sacred monuments alike. But that would be to forget the great enterprise to which he devoted himself in secret, unseen and unhonoured. For, from 1954 to 1967, he was engaged on the work that was to be his spiritual and artistic testament: the *Biblical Message*. As the curator of the Musée Chagall, where the *Message* is housed, explains, it 'stands, in the latter reaches of his career, as a synthesis of all the meaning embodied in his work, all the forms invented; and, looking forward, as a mine of new forms to feed into the other projects proposed to him: stained-glass windows, lithographs, tapestries and engravings'. In the light of this definition, it would seem that the *Biblical Message* served Chagall as a kind of ongoing laboratory experiment, an opportunity for pure research away from the applied pressures of public commissions.

At Cimiez, on a hill outside Nice, stands the small building which contains the whole of the *Biblical Message* – or rather one might say that the building itself is the message, so closely related are the works of art with the architectural concept and the leafy green surroundings of its site. There, since 1973, the visitor has been able to experience at once the unity and the multiplicity of Chagall's vision. Unity of theme and multiplicity of expression, stained glass, mosaics and tapestries coming together in a concerted display of visual virtuosity, in celebration of the Holy Scriptures. There are 17 large canvases, and also the 105 engravings of the Vollard suite, together with their copper plates, permitting an unrivalled insight into the complexities of Chagall's creative process.

It has been said that the physical and spiritual activity of painting is the best medicine there is. One is tempted to believe that may be true, given the number of painters who have worked right into old age, among them Renoir, Monet, Matisse, Bonnard, Picasso, Miró and Chirico. Yet the example of Chagall is hard to beat. He lived for nearly a century, painting and drawing every day of his life (he produced more than six hundred lithographs alone), supplying Pierre Matisse with a stream of major gouaches until shortly before his death, at his house in Vence, on 25 March 1985. Only three years before, an exhibition in New York had revealed to the public an entirely new style, using large expanses of colour wash, with the tenuous line of the drawing almost melting away into the watery surface of the damp paper. Never had 'the incredible lightness of being' (to borrow Milan Kundera's evocative title) been expressed in terms of such fragile transparency.

Human destiny often appears to be made up of a series of chance events, perhaps quite insignificant at the time, but which have the power to change the emphasis or the direction of a life, or disrupt it entirely. The century Chagall lived through was marked by political and social upheaval, obliging him to live a number of different lives as a permanent exile. But would he have been content in any case to live in quiet obscurity? Of course he did not choose war or revolution, but he had a remarkable knack of being in the right place at the right time, in pre-war Montparnasse, in Berlin with the Expressionists, in the heart of the revolutionary avant-garde in Russia, in New York with Stravinsky and Massine, and in Provence at the same time as Matisse and Picasso. The path his life followed coincided quite remarkably with the significant moments and triumphs of the advance of the modern movement.

It is as though his overwhelming urge to paint drew him almost instinctively to the places where the creative climate was most favourable to his own development. As though his painting, utterly subjective, and in no way capable of founding a school or attracting imitators, had no other destiny than to be itself, part of the great visual revolution of the twentieth century.

Michel Makarius

THE PLATES

My Fiancée with Black Gloves, 1909

Chagall was twenty-two when he fell in love with Bella Rosenfeld, in 1909. She was the daughter of an affluent family, and lived in an elegant house that was in utter contrast to his own modest dwelling in the suburbs. That is why this portrait of Chagall's future wife presents her as a somewhat remote and inaccessible figure, formally dressed in gloves and a hat. The dramatic collar of her tightly-fitting dress, and her haughty pose – she was a student at one of the best schools in Moscow – suggest that Chagall wanted to emphasize her theatricality.

There are numerous other paintings of Bella in existence, notably a nude study which Chagall hung on the wall of his room; he recalls in his memoirs that it brought complaints from his mother, shocked at such immodesty.

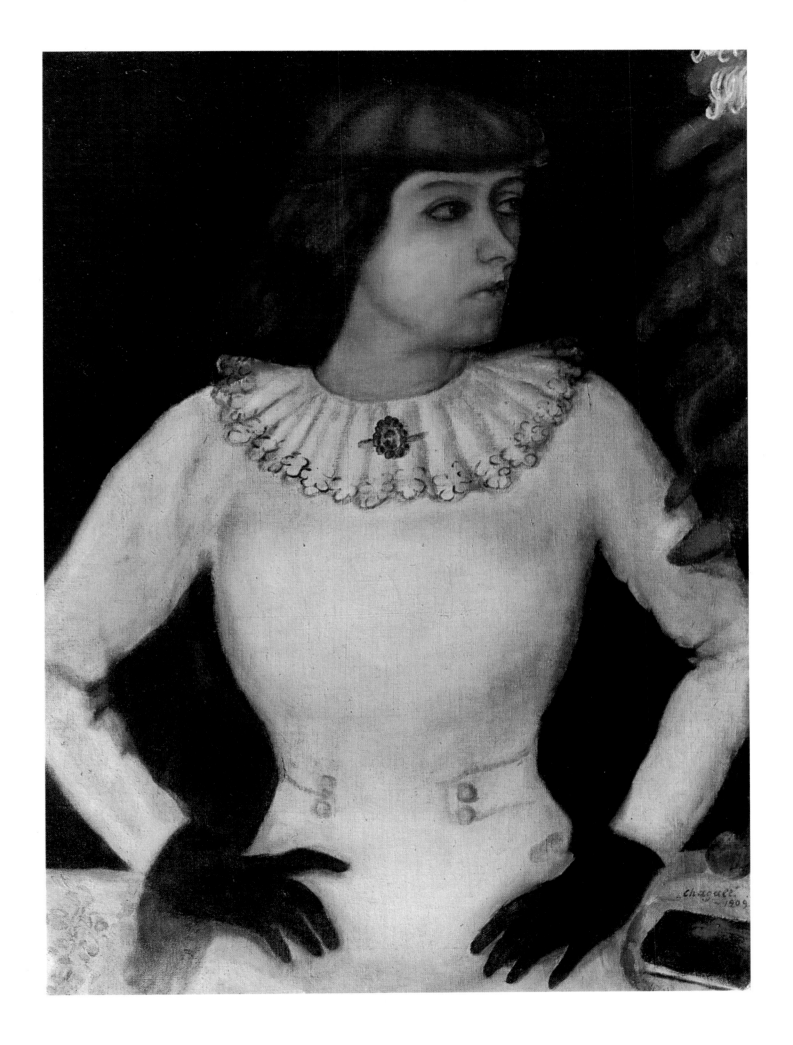

When he first arrived in Paris in 1910, Chagall occupied a furnished room just behind the Gare Montparnasse, lent to him by a Russian painter who was a relative of the writer Ilya Erenburg. He mingled with the cosmopolitan bohemian society who met in cafés like the Dôme and the Rotonde, and made himself known to the Russian contingent formed by the sculptors Zadkine, Lipchitz and Archipenko. (Soutine did not arrive until 1913.) In this period of poverty and struggle, when his only source of money was his patron Vinaver, Chagall was forced to use second-hand canvases. He did so for *The Studio*, which shows the painter's room at the Impasse du Maine, a painting of Bella hanging on the wall – *My Fiancée with Black Gloves*, which he had brought with him from Russia. Echoing the example of Matisse, Chagall gives free rein to his colour, and a pervasive green spreads over the walls and bed, blurring the distinction between vertical and horizontal planes. The carpet and the many framed paintings introduce a number of pictures-within-the-picture, tending to suppress the sense of depth. The armchairs have the friendly immediacy of Van Gogh's expressive evocations of familiar everyday objects. *The Studio* marks a complete break with Chagall's earlier Russian manner. His visits to the Louvre and the Salon d'Automne, and to the galleries of Durand-Ruel and Bernheim, were beginning to have their effect.

The Model, 1910

Of the pictures Chagall painted during his first months in Paris, *The Model* stands out most clearly as a work of transition. Its muted colours hark back to the mood of his Russian paintings, but the theme of the artist's model (here, rather curiously, occupying the painter's chair) is a complete departure from the scenes of everyday life that had hitherto provided him with his motifs.

Once again the setting is the painter's room – one recognizes the Louis-Philippe chair from *The Studio* – but now the objects are more important as structural elements than for themselves. The canvas on the easel and the armchair, both cut off by the edges of the picture, emphasize the lines of force in the composition. They provide a frame for the female figure, creating a mood of intimacy that is further reinforced by the floral motif on the walls, echoing the black pattern on the girl's blouse and the sequence of brush-marks she is making on the canvas. . . . Once again the overall scheme is highly reminiscent of Matisse, whose methods Chagall seems to have understood intuitively.

Head with Halo, 1911

This gouache, painted on a sheet of brown paper, illustrates a side of Chagall that in the past received little attention, although that omission has been rectified by the major exhibition of his drawings and watercolours held at the Pompidou Centre in Paris, in 1984. As *Head with Halo* shows, his work on paper has a sureness of touch one would not expect from the oils. The head is expressed in bold splashes of white, the brushwork rapid and deliberately crude, so that the final form is ambiguous, and it is not quite clear whether we are looking at a full-face portrait or a profile in which the right eye remains visible. There are other examples in Chagall's work of this theme of the dual-portrait, but this particular sketch is notable for its sensitive handling of the medium, and the striking use of the coloured paper surface as an integral element in the picture.

The Drunkard, 1911-12

In an earlier gouache version of this subject, Chagall used a fair amount of anecdotal detail to suggest an interior scene: playing cards lay on the table, together with a herring and a bowl of fruit, and there was even a cow peering through the window. When he returned to the theme in oils, however, he dispensed with the figurative background, attempting to structure space by means of colour alone, orchestrated in a geometric scheme that is reminiscent of the Cubist experiments of the Section d'Or group, or the paintings of Robert Delaunay. When *The Drunkard* was exhibited at the Salon des Indépendants of 1912, it looked entirely at home in the company of works by the orthodox Cubists.

Nevertheless, Chagall's attachment to this particular branch of the avant-garde was far from being unconditional. He said himself that Cubism was Realism 'with a sad face'. His own interest was in expressing the disturbance created by the eruption of imagination and feeling into the familiar world. Under the influence of alcohol, the drunkard of this picture is 'out of his senses'; his confusion expresses itself in the aggressive angularity of the objects (knife and bottle) and in the contrasts of yellow and red that slice diagonally across the canvas, to the point, Chagall explains, where it was the 'colour that dictated both the reversal of the chair and the cut-off head'. Here the specific cause of disequilibrium is drunkenness, but the picture also shows the beginnings of Chagall's attempts at bodily disintegration, a more permanent challenge to the laws of gravity and to the pedestrian reality of which they are a part.

To Russia, Asses, and Others, 1911-12

Painted on a remnant of cloth bought at the Bon Marché, *To Russia* is Chagall's first major painting from his time at La Ruche. He included a reproduction of it in the *Self-Portrait with Seven Fingers*, regarding the work as a sort of emblem of his attachment to Russian popular imagery, an antidote to all the new formal influences derived from the Parisian avant-garde. The canvas has been exhibited on many occasions, at the Salon des Indépendants of 1912, at the Der Sturm gallery in 1914, and as part of the major exhibition 'First papers of Surrealism', held in New York in 1941. It owes its curious title to the poet Blaise Cendrars, the allusion being to an avant-garde exhibition called 'The Donkey's Tail', held in Moscow in 1912; Chagall was among the contributors.

A preliminary gouache and drawing for *To Russia* reveal the complex gestation of the final canvas, and the gradual evolution of the imagery. What began as a realistic observation of rural life (a peasant woman going to milk her cow), passed through many stages to end as a statement with all the resonance of myth; the cow that is the source of nourishment to its people has certain parallels with the wolf who reared Romulus and Remus, and it also carries echoes of the Egyptian goddess Hator, often represented as the heavenly cow who gave birth to the universe. The night sky – a later addition, suggested by the eclipse that occurred in Europe in 1912 – serves to reinforce the picture's sense of mysterious significance, so that each detail – angel, bucket, animal, human figure and head – seems to stand out like a sign against the strange light of the shooting-stars in the sky. If the picture grew out of the humblest activities of the farmer's life, as a sort of primitivist manifesto – an aspect of Chagall that appealed strongly to Gauguin – it found its final form in the transfiguration of these activities into symbols.

Homage to Apollinaire, 1912

The poet Apollinaire was a good friend to the painters of his day and only too willing to set pen to paper in support of their latest artistic theories. He met Chagall in 1913 and was quickly won over by the qualities of imagination shown in his 'supranatural' art. *Homage to Apollinaire* was Chagall's acknowledgment of the debt he owed to the poet and to the three other friends whose names are set, with his, in a square at the foot of the painting, surrounding a heart pierced by an arrow. They are: Riciotto Canudo, who admired Chagall's work from the first, Herwarth Walden, the German dealer and publisher who arranged his one-man show at the Berlin gallery Der Sturm, in 1914, and Blaise Cendrars, the footloose author of *Prose du Transsibérien*, who proved marvellously adept at inventing titles for his Russian friend's paintings. It has been suggested that the four names have another significance as well, being phonetic references to the four elements: thus Apollinaire would stand for 'air', Canudo for 'water' (*eau*, in French), Cendrars for 'fire' and Walden for 'earth' (*Wald* being the German word meaning 'forest'). Be that as it may, it is certainly true that the geometrical form of the figures, and their position within the circle, raise the canvas to a level of abstraction where forms acquire the hidden significance of symbols. The circle has cosmological overtones, and is an image of totality and the relentless passing of time, the figures around its edge suggesting those on a clock-face. . . . But it is in the representation of Adam and Eve as a single body, dividing into two at the level of the genitals, that *Homage to Apollinaire* reveals itself above all as an allegory of the nature of love, with its power to unite two in one. Such treatment of human figures as bloodless symbols is quite exceptional in Chagall's *oeuvre*; were it not for the evidence of preparatory drawings, it would be impossible to detect that the circle derives out of the image of a coiled snake. One must assume that the unusual abstraction of *Homage to Apollinaire* was intended specifically as a tribute to the avant-garde tendencies of Apollinaire, that the letters and numbers introduced into the composition are a conscious nod in the direction of the Cubists, and the contrasting zones of flat colour a reference to Orphism.

Adam and Eve, 1912

In 1912 Cubism was at the height of its influence. Braque and Picasso's experiments with form were by now in the public domain, and a whole host of painters were trying to adapt the new approach to their personal vision. At the Académie de la Palette, of which Le Fauconnier had been appointed director, Chagall attended the studio run by Metzinger, a member of the Section d'Or group, who set himself the task of codifying the new pictorial language. *Adam and Eve* is unique in Chagall's *oeuvre* in its full-blooded attempt to come to terms with the lessons of this radical reinterpretation of perception. The two bodies are fragmented into multiple planes and dispersed over the whole picture surface, in such a way that they are almost beyond recognition. Like Fernand Léger, Robert Delaunay or the Italian Futurists, in their different ways, Chagall was responding to the prevailing aesthetic of the artistic world of his time. But in his case it was to be no more than a brief experiment, with no lasting consequences. Chagall's painting was only fleetingly affected by fashion. And even here he demonstrates his independence from the accepted iconographical models of the avant-garde, choosing a traditional motif rooted in his biblical heritage.

The Pinch of Snuff, 1912

In *The Pinch of Snuff*, Chagall attempts to convey the peculiar atmosphere associated with the Jewish religion, rooted as it is in the study of the Scriptures and Holy Books. The luminosity and warmth of the yellow stands out brilliantly against the severe black of the man's robe (he is presumably a rabbi), heightening the mood of devout concentration. At first sight, the trivial gesture of taking snuff seems to belie the religious character of the picture, but that is to misunderstand Chagall's intentions. He wants us to experience the reading of the Talmud as an almost physical reality, symbolized by that apparently insignificant act: it is as though, as he inhales his tobacco, the man absorbs the savour of the text before him. We know that such scenes impressed themselves upon the notice of the young Chagall, for he refers in his memoirs to his father's habit 'of turning to his neighbours and asking them to remain silent during prayers, or asking them for a pinch of snuff.'

The subject was obviously of particular significance to Chagall for he produced several variations on the theme, one gouache, two oils and, as late as 1924, a watercolour. In the gouache, the Hebrew inscription in the centre of the Star of David means 'life', while in the later versions this is changed to 'death', probably in reference to the tragic ending of a novella by the great Yiddish writer I. L. Peretz – which Chagall must certainly have known as he illustrated a number of his other tales. The text visible in the open book in the foreground has been identified as Yiddish, and X-ray examination has revealed that some of the script has been overpainted. While the body of the text appears to be meaningless, the words.'Segal Moshe' have been reconstructed, and it is thought this may be an anagram of the artist's name. Thus a picture steeped in the traditions of devout Judaism turns out to be full of unexpected esoteric references.

Self-Portrait with Seven Fingers, 1912-13

When Chagall moved to a studio at La Ruche, early in 1912, he found himself in the society of people of his own kind. Just to be there, in a community of artists, was a confirmation of his destiny as a painter. But as he worked in Vaugirard, in the heart of Paris, all his thoughts and feelings were concentrated on Russia, where Bella was waiting for him. The *Self-Portrait* provides the perfect illustration of his dilemma: behind him, through the window, Paris and the Eiffel Tower, the emblem of modernity; facing him on the easel, in a mist of nostalgia, the church and houses of Vitebsk; and, between the two, reflecting a third aspect of his personality, the names of the two towns written in Hebrew. Art seems to be the only way of reconciling the contradictory elements of his existence. The canvas on the easel, the recently-painted *To Russia, Asses and Others*, suggests that the only meaningful subject is Mother Russia. Yet Chagall himself is wearing a suit of a Cubist or Futurist design, with a little coloured-paper collage on the lapel. Is that not an implicit recognition that his new artistic personality has emerged out of his contacts with the Parisian avant-garde?

Self-Portrait with Seven Fingers is above all an affirmation of the artist's capacity to transfigure reality, using the exceptional power he has, quite literally, at his fingertips. The source of his magic is the colour set out on the palette, itself forming a picture to echo the views of Paris and Vitebsk. With his transfigured hand, the artist appears to demonstrate its limitless possibilities.

Paris through the Window, 1913

By the time his first visit came to an end, Chagall had grown so fond of the French capital that he said, quite simply: 'Paris, you are my second Vitebsk.' It seemed a long time ago that he had arrived as a young emigré at the Gare du Nord and, terrified by the anonymity of the big city, confessed 'only the vast distance separating Paris from my home town prevented me from returning there at once, or at the most in a week or a month'. It was also a long time since the townscape of Paris had been relegated to a small corner of his canvas, as in *Self-Portrait with Seven Fingers*. Now, in *Paris through the Window*, Chagall demonstrated the affection he felt for the city that had taken him in and given him a double sense of belonging. Perhaps that is the significance of the Janus-like head looking two ways at once, towards Paris and out into the distance? In any case, it is entirely consistent with the duality of Chagall's universe, with its linked contrasts of dream and reality, present and past, human and animal, visible and invisible. Another example is the cat with a human head, a fabulous or mythical creature who balances on the window-sill, guarding the frontier between indoors and outdoors; or the upside-down train – an allusion to the underground railway; or the parachutist who floats in a sky coloured with the blue, white and red of France, the sky Chagall was shortly to leave behind when he set out for Germany and Russia.

Over Vitebsk, 1914

This painting could perfectly well be a naturalistic scene of Vitebsk in the snow, were it not for the mysterious figure rising up from behind the Ilitch church, like a kind of flying tramp. The explanation of his presence lies in Jewish culture, and in particular in the Yiddish language, where the word for a beggar who goes from door to door may be literally translated as a man 'who walks over the town'. Victims of persecution and pogroms, the Jews of Eastern Europe recognized themselves in this wandering beggar with his bundle slung over one shoulder. . . .

Or it may also be a reference to the prophet Elias, who is often described as arriving like an unexpected visitor in one of his many disguises: Chagall imagines him 'looking like a poor old man, a stooping beggar with a pack on his back and a stick in his hand' – here he wears too a Russian cap.

Over Vitebsk was painted soon after Chagall arrived back in his home town. It was bought by the collector Kagan-Chabchaj, who already owned a number of canvases by Chagall and planned to found a Jewish museum (a project which failed to materialize because of the October Revolution).

Jew in Black and White, 1914

'Another old man passes our houses. Grey hair, surly-looking. A pack on his back. . . . Listen – I tell him – rest your legs. Sit down. That's it. You don't mind, do you? Have a good rest. I'll give you twenty kopeks. Just put on my father's prayer robe and sit down. – Did you see my picture of an old man praying? That's him.' That is Chagall's description in *My Life* of how he found his model for this picture, an authentic wandering Jew, whose features showed the marks of fatigue and suffering that epitomized the condition of the Jews in Central Europe. Yet the face shown here would not have that wider significance of an archetype if it were not for the prayer shawl which, under Chagall's expert handling, becomes a quasi-abstract geometric form, corresponding to the cuboid form of the *tephillim* (small leather boxes containing fragments of the Scriptures written on parchment) attached to the man's forehead. The painting as a whole is lent added force by its colour scheme, restricted to the black and white of the traditional shawl. Having once succeeded in capturing the image of the Jew at his devotions, as it has been handed down from generation to generation (see photo), Chagall went on to produce several variations on the theme.

Feast Day, 1914

This picture is directly inspired by the feast of the Sukkut (or of the Tabernacles), which celebrates the crossing of the desert by the Jewish people. The rabbi wears the *tallit*, or long prayer shawl, and, following the prescriptions in Leviticus, holds in his hands the ritual objects: the citron (a sort of inedible lemon) and the palm. Chagall departs from tradition, however, in showing the figure at the entrance of a building, since the custom for the feast of the Tabernacles was to construct canopies of branches. Set in a bare geometric space, the rabbi with his attributes bears a certain similarity to scenes from the life of St Francis painted by Giotto, whom we know from *My Life* Chagall admired greatly.

In its subject matter, *Feast Day* belongs with the series of *The Pinch of Snuff*, *Jew at Prayer*, *Jew in Green* and *Jew in Red*, all painted in 1914. Yet the gravity of these paintings is replaced here by a far cooler appraisal of reality. Balanced on the rabbi's head is a tiny miniature of himself, a figure oblivious to his surroundings, like an ironic comment on the proceedings. The solemn presence of the lemon and the mini-rabbi thus lend this ritual scene an element of the mocking self-deprecation that is the prerogative of Jewish humour.

Jew in Green, 1914

Rabbis, wandering Jews peddling the holy word, devout beggars – Chagall painted numerous such quasi-mythical figures in the years 1912–14, representing them always as gaunt, bearded old men impelled by their religious faith. Yet the various portraits are far from uniform. Each has its own particular mood, dominated by affection and familiarity (*The Pinch of Snuff*), respect and worship (*Jew at Prayer*), or humour and irony (*Feast Day*). Of them all, *Jew in Green* is the most plainly tragic. The man's green face and yellow beard seem as old as time, like the ancient sacred text carved into the surface at his back. Chagall recalls the care he had to take with these devout old men when he wanted to paint them, well aware that he risked offending against the ban on representation. With the *Jew in Green*, known to be the preacher from Slousk, no such problems arose: 'He came, sat down on a chair, and at once fell asleep.' As Chagall paints him, his weariness is that of a whole people condemned to servitude and discrimination.

The Birthday, 1915

The Birthday celebrates Chagall's reunion with Bella, whom he married in Vitebsk on 25 July 1915. It is the first use of the famous motif of lovers floating in the air – to which Chagall would return again and again. The highly improbable stance adopted by the figures illustrates, both literally and metaphorically, the transports of love, but the interior is teeming with realistic detail. Chagall rented a room from a policeman, and that is what we see, faithfully reproduced: Bella's scarves hung up on the wall, the Ilitch church through the window (it also figured in *Over Vitebsk*), the *fortochka*, a small opening in the top of the window that is a typical feature of Russian houses, even the birthday cake on the table.

In later years, Bella recalled the happy days she spent with Chagall in Vitebsk, her memories inextricably entwined with the painting the couple took back with them to Paris: 'Suddenly you lifted me up off the floor and, all by yourself, you carried me up with you, as though the little room was too small for you, you leapt, you stretched up with your whole length and you flew to the ceiling. Your head was turned back to me- and you turned mine up to face yours. . . .'

The Reclining Poet, 1915

A work expressive of peace and contentment, *The Reclining Poet* was executed during Chagall's honeymoon with Bella, in the country near Vitebsk. He tells us he painted exactly what he saw: 'Woods, pine trees, solitude. The moon behind the forest, the pig in the sty, the horse through the window, in the fields. The lilac sky.' The world presents itself to him with the obviousness and simplicity of happiness itself; at the same time, each element – meadow, birch tree, pine, horse, pig – seems to have been put there by the painter to make up an ideal landscape, like an illustrated guide to the joys of country life. In much the same way does a poet use words to paint a picture of the world, and so he is seen here too, lying flat on the grass, sunk in a deep reverie. His position corresponds to the base of the canvas, which is square, reinforcing the sense of artificiality. Thus the scene is both real and a function of the poet's wandering imagination, with which the painter identifies. It may well be that Chagall painted what he saw – the dusky light, silence gathering like dew over the meadow – but then, to him, nature was already a miraculous apparition.

Window in the Country, 1915

In the summer of 1915, following their marriage, Bella and Marc Chagall went to stay in a *dacha* in Zaolcha, outside Vitebsk. Through the window, in this drawing we see the same birch wood that is glimpsed in *The Reclining Poet*. It is clear that Chagall now wants nothing more than to represent the real world, just as it appears to him; he is back in Russia, so his windows no longer open onto scenes of nostalgia, expressing the longing to escape, they open onto the living, present world that is once again his. But this is no disenchanted Realism, far from it; although there are prosaic domestic objects – a plate upside-down upon another, a jug, a sugar-bowl – the atmosphere is intimate and lyrical. The couple's two profiles, peering through the gap left by the raised curtain, transform the scene outside into a kind of impromptu performance, an occasion for surreptitious enjoyment. It is an image of shared absorption in a miraculous world, no doubt a conscious reversal, on Chagall's part, of one of his favourite motifs, the ambivalent two-faced Janus. All his compositional skill goes into the subtle interaction between interior and external world – the latter as private and enclosed as the former. From the window-sill up to the sky, in the curtain and the bark of the birches, there are a thousand shades of grey, imparting depth and warmth. There is hint too of a Cubist-inspired fragmentation of the planes, in the folds of the curtain – the strategic element of the whole composition – and in the treatment of the grass and foliage, reflected in the miraculous transparency of the glass.

The Mirror, 1915

In both theme and treatment, *The Mirror* reflects a side of Chagall that is rarely seen. There is no hint of his usual motley palette in the flat expanses of green and mauve that form the background, against which the highly-wrought decoration of the mirror-frame stands out sharply, creating a picture-within-a-picture. The strange column that forms the standard of the oil-lamp seems to set up a dialogue with the moulding on the frame, so that the scale of the painting appears suddenly in doubt: they might be architectural details on a building. The impression of monumentality is reinforced by the tiny figure asleep at the foot of the mirror. The image of the lamp, captured in the illusory depth of the mirror, is even more disturbing. It seems not so much a reflection as an emanation of the mirror itself, generated by its own light. Chagall always had a love of magic and mystification, but here the stark simplicity of the image presents a genuine enigma.

The Grey House, 1917

In the summer of 1917, Chagall again found himself in Vitebsk. It was the opportunity to paint his beloved town once more and try to capture something of its essence. As in *The Blue House* of the same period, a contrast is made between the gracious centre of the town, dominated by the Baroque towers of the monastery, and a simple wooden hut, its walls all askew; on the fence are graffiti, further underlining the realism of the detail, and above is an expanse of threatening sky. In the foreground, a casual passer-by leans against a bank of heaped-up billets, rendered here as semi-abstract geometric forms. Even when painting from the motif, in a broadly realistic vein, Chagall could not restrain his invention, or resist the impulse to 'stage-manage' a landscape.

The Cemetery Gate, 1917

Here Chagall is less interested in the theme of the Jewish cemetery, with its tangle of graves, than he is in exploring the notion of Resurrection. The text on the gateway is – untypically – a quotation from the prophet Ezekiel: 'Behold, O my people, I will open up your graves, and cause you to come up out of your graves, and bring you into the land of Israel.' Covered in inscriptions, not all of which can be deciphered, the two pillars look like the rolls of the Torah.

A sense of upward movement fills the sky, creating a mood of religious exaltation comparable to that evoked, in another guise, in the series of rabbis painted in 1914; a complex of faceted prisms, somewhat reminiscent of Larionov's Rayonism, binds together the various elements in a tortuous rhythm, suggestive of spiritual agony. The tree, symbol of life and freedom, expresses the living reality of Resurrection.

Composition with Circles and Goat, 1917

Painted in oils on cardboard, *Composition with Circles and Goat* belongs to the period when Chagall was involved in stage-design, specifically for Sholem Aleichem's *The Lie*. One of his sketches for the production shows a figure disappearing behind a large screen, rather in the way, in this picture, a foot and half a goat appear in the aperture of the yellowish rectangle – which, judging by the altered perspective at the base, has roughly the depth of a panel, or stage-flat. The goat had a special significance for Chagall, who used it in many of his theatre designs and in numerous other sketches and canvases.

Modest and unpretentious, *Composition with Circles and Goat* is executed with great delicacy, the unemphatic line denying narrative content and concentrating attention on qualities of paint and surface. As in *Collage* or *Cubist Landscape*, the image takes second place to purely pictorial considerations, making it an untypical example in Chagall's iconography.

The Promenade, 1917

The Birthday showed the lovers defying for the first time the laws of gravity, rising up together to the ceiling. Now they are out of doors – from the flask of wine, the glass and the tablecloth, with its Matisse-like surface ornamentation, we can see they are having a picnic in the country. Marc holds Bella by the hand, but she is not standing at his side, she is tugging at his arm, soaring up into the air like a kite. The image of weightlessness, used with equal success in *Above the Town* and *Double Portrait with Wineglass*, both painted shortly after the Revolution, carries with it a poetic charge of overwhelming simplicity and power. If, as André Breton believed, 'only with him did metaphor make its triumphal entry onto the scene of modern art', then this image of the flying lovers is the perfect symbol of the delights of shared happiness, expressing both the ecstasy of physical fulfilment and a more cosmic sense of being at one with nature. All one might add is that the various elements – sky, landscape and human figures – are rendered in a style derived from Cubism and Futurism, the cloud, the meadows, the houses and the couple's clothes being expressed in a scheme of interlinked geometrical forms. The only line of force is the strong rising diagonal formed by the extended arm, which goes right off the top of the canvas, suggesting an exuberance that cannot be contained within this single moment in time.

Above the Town, 1917-18

Bella and Marc are floating in the sky over the town of Vitebsk. Chagall never tired of painting the place where he was born and brought up, and to which he remained fiercely loyal: 'Now I am here. It is my town, my tomb. Here I open up in the evening and at night, like the tobacco plant (which opens its petals in darkness). By the grace of God, I am working,' he wrote to the director of his gallery in Petrograd. Equally, it was because of his known attachment to his home town that Lunacharsky appointed him director of the School of Fine Arts, in 1918. Vitebsk gave Chagall his roots, a fixed point of reality to which he would always return, tempering the flights of his soaring imagination. On the rare occasions when he painted scenes of the countryside (*The Reclining Poet, Window in the Country*) without that restraint, nature tended to appear far more as a reflection of his own subjective consciousness. In *Above the Town*, the jagged wooden fencing, seen previously in *The Grey House*, imparts a strong horizontal rhythm to the landscape, echoed by the line of the floating couple. The canvas was exhibited at the time of Chagall's official nomination as director, together with the two other major canvases that sum up this interlude in Vitebsk: *The Promenade* and *Double Portrait with Wineglass*. *Above the Town* was among the last of Chagall's paintings to be acquired by the Russian state, in 1921.

Double Portrait with Wineglass, 1917-18

The *Double Portrait* is not really about the miracle of levitation, rather it suggests high spirits, the sheerly pleasurable sensations produced, perhaps, by a glass of wine or the gentle breeze wafted by a fan. The couple's light-heartedness is plain to see; indeed, their lack of gravity is represented physically, in the stance they have adopted, as well as in their visible delight at the trick they are playing on us, the spectators. The tall, narrow picture, with its extended vertical, is like a mocking echo of our own verticality as we stand there looking at the pair; Marc appears to raise his glass to us in a toast, while, lower down, Bella's single eye meets ours with an infinitely knowing look. The fan is like the magical source of the Cubist structure that unfurls over the surface, fragmenting the planes. Although the dark green waters of the Dvina serve to anchor the painting in reality, Bella's slender mauve leg sets up a diagonal that rises right up through the picture, to be completed finally in the mauve of the angelic creature descending from the skies – identified as representing Ida, the Chagall's newly-born child. The diagonal not only links the man and the woman, it also divides the sky into two distinct zones of colour, as though at the behest of the couple who are masters of their universe.

Cubist Landscape, 1919

Ironic in tone, *Cubist Landscape* comments obliquely on Chagall's differences with Malevich, during the time he was in charge of the Vitebsk School of Fine Arts. The facts, briefly, are that the leader of the Suprematists took advantage of his director's absence to put up a banner proclaiming the existence of a new Suprematist Academy, replacing the old Free Academy; Chagall's resignation followed, in 1920. *Cubist Landscape* was Chagall's way of parodying Malevich's formalist theories and, more generally, all the squabbles over aesthetics that divided the revolutionary artists. Thus, the School building here is largely obliterated by semi-circular geometric forms such as appeared in innumerable avant-garde pictures of the time; the introduction of surfaces representing wood, fabric or paper is an allusion to French Cubism and to the debate among Russian artists over the need to bring new materials into painting. Chagall regarded these arguments as sterile disputes over theory and preferred to adopt an attitude of humorous detachment, as we may infer from his inclusion here of an endless stream of doodles in Roman and Cyrillic lettering, spelling out his own name, and the irreverent interjections of a goat and a little man holding an umbrella.

At the same time, *Cubist Landscape* demonstrates the ease with which Chagall was able to absorb outside influences and incorporate elements of the new artistic vocabulary into his own work – as, for example, in his sketches for the Jewish Theatre.

Introduction to the Jewish Theatre, 1920

Nothing could have suited Chagall better than the commission he was given in 1920, by the director Granowsky, to decorate the auditorium of the Jewish Theatre in Moscow. It was the perfect outlet for the fantastic imaginings of a painter reared in the Hasidic traditions of the miraculous. Chagall had already had some contact with the stage, having designed sets and costumes for a number of Gogol's plays (large numbers of these sketches have been preserved) and also for three 'miniatures' by the Yiddish writer Sholem Aleichem. But with *Introduction to the Jewish Theatre*, theatre itself is the theme. It is a monumental work, 4 by 12 metres, filling the whole of one wall, complemented by four panels, on the opposite wall, dedicated to the arts: *Music, Dance, Theatre* and *Literature*, these surmounted by a frieze entitled *The Table for the Wedding Feast*. We know from a contemporary source, Lubomirsky, that the descriptive detail of the vast decorative scheme had an influence 'that manifested itself not only in terms of stage décors, make-up techniques and costumes, but also in the performances given by actors. . . .'

Introduction to the Jewish Theatre included real personalities in its cast of characters. On the left is the figure of Chagall himself, lifted up by his friend, the critic Effross, who first introduced him to Granowsky; the latter too appears, facing a dwarf, and the principal actor Michoëls is shown spinning like a top. Individual figures apart, the composition is a kaleidoscope of activity, as the poet Marcel Schwob describes: 'It is a vast fresco in which all the usual theatrical characters appear to have sprung into collective life, some walking on their hands, others advancing or leaping through the air in a rhythm that catches up in it the other more conventional-looking characters to create just that mood of poetic truth that is characteristic of the drama.' (*Chagall et l'âme juive*)

Along the twelve metres of the canvas's length, Chagall develops a choreographed movement that is punctuated by abstract geometric forms, echoing and restating the rhythms of the traditional Hasidic dance; it is a remarkable achievement, and one of the finest expressions of the renaissance of Jewish culture that accompanied the Revolution.

Collage, 1921

Although collage was an unusual technique for Chagall, this example shows that he understood its particular requirements. Exploiting the qualities of each element to the full, he makes the centre of the composition a dark-coloured diagonal of marbled bookbinding paper, which then dictates the position of the other cut-outs – one of which is a piece from the programme for the opening night of the Jewish Theatre. The Hebrew script written in the triangle formed by the flap of an envelope means 'The Great Sage'. Chagall allows his background surface plenty of space to breathe, and makes each element a self-contained, almost tactile entity within the whole. The composition would not have been unworthy of the master of collage Kurt Schwitters, who admired Chagall, and in 1919 dedicated a poem to him. Although Schwitters is not referred to by name, this was undoubtedly Chagall's response.

צדק

21 г.

XIII ВЫ...ЕНТРОСЕКЦ...
...ОМПРОСА.

...съ художника
...ОКА ШАГАЛА.

...ейский театр.   5. Литература—
                         6. Свадебный стол
                         7. Любовь на сцене
                         8. Плафон.

...и зрительного зала сербского государствен-
...камерного театра (Б. Чернышевский, д. 12.)
...Открыта для осмотра с 3 час. до 5 час.
                    Вход свободный

...турно просветительны...
Комитеты и У...

1920   Marc Chagall

The Window on the Island of Bréhat, 1924

In June 1924, Chagall spent a peaceful holiday with his family at the Ile de Bréhat in Brittany. Now he looked at the French landscape with eyes undimmed by nostalgia for his native land. In this picture there is an atmosphere of serenity, and the window is thrown wide open to reveal a landscape stretching down to the sea; silvery grey light fills the room. Although the window frame marks a division between the private world indoors and the objective reality of the world outside, yet there is a continuity of mood between the two; the reflection of the landscape in the window-panes matches the colour of the sky outside. In another picture painted at this time, Chagall showed his daughter Ida sitting at the same window; although her body faces into the room, her head is turned to look outwards – emphasizing the painter's own new openness to the beauties of the French landscape.

The Lion Grown Old, 1926-27

In 1926, Chagall presented the publisher and art dealer Ambroise Vollard with the idea of an illustrated edition of La Fontaine's *Fables*. Vollard was intrigued by what he knew of Chagall's work and offered a commission. Almost at once, voices were raised in protest. How could an artist steeped in a tradition of Russian fantasy hope to convey the classical spirit of such a quintessentially French writer as La Fontaine, the glory of the Grand Siècle? Vollard stood by his guns and defended his choice publicly – demonstrating, not for the first time, the soundness of his instincts. Chagall's imagery betrayed an empathy with the animal world that went beyond mere affection and familiarity. What is more, he had been reared in the oriental tradition of the 'fabulous tale', and his painting was rooted in popular sources, in the very idiom and proverbs of the language – making it what the Italian art historian Argan called a true visual 'fabulation'.

Chagall went on to produce more than a hundred gouaches of wonderful freedom, endearing in their almost childlike simplicity, and full of humorous touches that are expressed very often by the interpolation of an unexpected splash of colour – as here in the frisky blue donkey who disturbs the harmonious gravity of the ochres and browny reds.

If Chagall scorns a too literal interpretation of the tales, for the most part simply uninterested in the details of the narrative or the precise moral attached to it, he succeeds miraculously in capturing the sheer verve and wit of this amused contemplation of the human race, its foibles reflected – to the evident delight of writer and painter alike – among the denizens of the animal kingdom.

The Dream, 1927

Upturned on the back of a quadruped who is neither donkey nor hare, a young girl gazes up, not at the sky, but an upside-down nocturnal landscape, completed by the white disc of the moon in the bottom left hand corner. The confusion of above and below, and the incongruous presence of the long-eared animal bearing his strange burden, make it clear that we are in the unconscious world of the dream. This is unusual in Chagall's work; while the unconscious plays its part in the workings of the imagination, the mood here is quite at variance with the distinctive blend of unreality and realism we see elsewhere in Chagall.

If *The Dream* is unusual too in its colours and in the freedom of the handling (close to that of the gouaches for the *Fables*), the theme of riding is one the painter turned to on several occasions. His equestriennes on their circus horses are like the day-time counterparts of the figures in *The Dream*. The circus was another magic world in which there existed a complicity between women and animals, and it provided Chagall with an inexhaustible source of inspiration: trapeze artists, clowns and acrobats were the subjects of a whole series of paintings in the late twenties.

The Russian Village, 1929

In this painting Chagall succeeds in making it look entirely natural for a sleigh to take off from the ground and fly through the air. True, Christmas scenes have familiarized us with the idea of an airborne traveller looking down on sleepy villages in the snow, but there is more to the picture than that. The snow-covered street that winds between the houses creates an illusion of depth, so that the upward flight of the sleigh into the sky becomes simply a natural extension of the track zig-zagging through the village, echoed by the angles of the roofs. The classic effects of perspective and the choice of a rather neutral palette, heightened only by the dark red of a wooden façade, all contribute to giving *The Russian Village* the appearance of a Realist work; within this context, the winter travellers simply take their place.

Noah's Drunkenness, 1931

After the series based on La Fontaine's *Fables*, Vollard asked Chagall to produce illustrations for an edition of the Bible. In so doing he opened up an extraordinarily fertile vein for the painter, and one that was to dominate the rest of his career. First, the etchings themselves were started in 1931 but not completed until 1956 (to be published by Tériade in the following year, Vollard having died in the interim). Then, quite apart from this series of 66 illustrations, and numerous paintings, there followed the stained-glass windows for Metz Cathedral and the *Biblical Message*, created in Nice in the period 1969–73, further evidence of Vollard's prescience in suggesting this particular source of motifs to Chagall.

Before embarking on the major project of illustrating the Scriptures, Chagall visited Palestine with his family, experiencing for himself the atmosphere of the Holy Land and absorbing the qualities of the light and landscape.

Noah's Drunkenness is based on the incident when the patriarch unwisely overindulged in wine and threw off all his clothes; one of his sons averted his eyes and covered his nakedness with a garment. The details of the scene, Noah lying there red-faced with two flasks, one already emptied, and the son's dismayed reactions, are taken directly from the Biblical text. But, beyond that, the deliberately rough outlines of the figures and the scribbled colour of the coat and backdrop of the landscape, are intended to convey a sort of primitivism appropriate to the age of Genesis.

Solitude, 1933

Clasping the rolls of the Torah, an old Jew is sitting sunk in his thoughts. At his side, a young cow lies on the grass. The picture's charm derives out of its silent juxtaposition of complementary motifs, human meditation having its counterpart in the ingenuous presence of the ruminant beast, even though no communication exists between them. The Jew sits wrapped in his shawl, oblivious even to the angel in the sky. Chagall presented the painting to the Tel-Aviv museum – perhaps he did so because its protagonist was dreaming of the Promised Land? Seen in this light, his solitude is a product of his vision of eternity, against which everything else pales, becomes a mere background, like the roofs of Vitebsk on the horizon. As for the animal, its whiteness suggesting innocence, it symbolizes the endurance of the species from the time of the Creation. The weary, melancholic man and the patient animal, both of them exiles in this world, are enveloped in the same tranquil aura of sanctity.

Study for The Revolution, 1937

Twenty years after the October Revolution, Chagall felt the need to return to the events he had lived through so closely. At a time when, in Paris, artists were full of revolutionary theories and debates about political engagement, when the Spanish Civil War mobilized a whole generation and Picasso was moved to paint *Guernica*, the former commissar of the School of Fine Arts in Vitebsk began work on a vast fresco showing a people in revolt, artists, musicians and tumblers congregating around the figure of Lenin. But what a picture of Lenin this is, not the usual respectful official portrait by any means. He is shown as an acrobat, feet in the air, supporting himself by one hand on a table (on which leans the *alter ego* of the old Jew from the picture *Solitude*). Of course, the handstand performed by the leader of the Bolsheviks symbolizes the social and political transformations of the Revolution, and by showing him surrounded by a group of artists Chagall indicates at once where his sympathies lie. Yet, although Lenin is the central figure, the composition is separated into two distinct zones: on the one side is a dense crowd of people, while on the other, around a large disc (which had a samovar at its centre in a preliminary drawing), is an assembly of artists, among them a painter at his easel and a violinist, and also, lower down, perching on a roof (an image of childhood) a couple with a child. The two groups are entirely distinct, even though they are watching the same scene. It is as though Chagall wanted to show that the Revolution, intended to be the salvation of the individual as well as the means of rescuing the masses from oppression, did not in fact succeed in reconciling private aspirations with social ideals.

It is no accident, then, that Chagall came to regard his own attempt to paint the Revolution as a failure. Now we have only a small sketch to remind us of the gigantic canvas which, in 1943, Chagall cut into sections; the two pictures thus created bore titles more in keeping with the reality: *Liberation* and *Resistance*. Chagall's own admission of defeat clearly reflected the failure of the Revolution itself, which began by according full citizenship to the Jews and injecting a spirit of unprecedented freedom into the land of the Czars, only to degenerate into a dictatorship, of whose dangers Chagall was only too aware.

The Blue Angel, 1938

Chagall frequently painted the figure of an angel appearing in the sky, as if interceding on behalf of the invisible realm of the imagination. In *The Blue Angel* the effect is not unlike a Christian Annunciation scene, except that the heavenly messenger is kneeling before the offering of a magnificent bouquet of flowers. In the background, an artist stands at his easel painting crescent moons, and human figures float in space, seen in profile. The picture is a further affirmation of Chagall's optimism, even in the face of the increasing perilousness of the times, reflected in other paintings. Quite simply, it shows his determination to continue to paint flowers.

Jacob Wrestling with the Angel, 1938/68

Chagall's commitment to religious painting achieved its culmination with the opening in 1969 of a small museum in Nice, designed to house *The Biblical Message*. For the painter it was the realization of a dream that had haunted him since the fifties, in fact from the time when he had begun to think of his work in terms of cycles. Here the pictures, brought together in a place specifically designed for them, could achieve a cumulative expressive power that transcended their individual impact, the architecture as much a part of the *Message* as the works themselves. Although the museum is not a place of worship, it stands as a monument of impressive spirituality.

The oil painting of *Jacob Wrestling with the Angel* belongs to the cycle of *The Biblical Message*, and was probably completed in the sixties – although the dating is imprecise and Chagall certainly explored the theme many years before that. Even though the incident recorded is of a solitary struggle in semi-darkness, Chagall takes the liberty here of introducing a crowd of onlookers and a number of figures from his private mythology – presumably because of his paramount desire to show the people as witnesses to biblical events. In a number of pen-and-ink drawings and watercolours preceding the final version in oils by ten years or more, the traditional iconography is respected, the struggle being shown simply as a contrast of light and dark, very much in the spirit of the Rembrandt of this subject Chagall saw in Berlin.

White Crucifixion, 1938

In this painting are reflected the political realities of pre-war Europe: the rise of the Nazis in Germany, the pogroms in Poland, the undercurrent of anti-Semitic feeling in France – all directed against the Jews. By virtue of its sheer size, its graphic depiction of destruction and the central motif of Christ on the Cross, the picture has the character of a terrible warning. The inscription in Hebrew over Christ's head, which reads 'Jesus of Nazareth, King of the Jews', and the white and black-striped prayer shawl wrapped around the body, are explicit reminders that, even on the Cross, Christ was a son of Israel. It is as such that he is placed here, at the centre of scenes of cruel injury being inflicted on his people.

A blazing synagogue is attacked by a brown-shirted Nazi, houses are burned out, men flee in all directions before the threat of an army advancing under the red flag. . . . Far from being alone in his suffering, as Christian iconography would dictate, Christ remains a man among men. As Franz Meyer explains: '. . . any notion of salvation is absent from Chagall's conception of Christ.'

The scattered scenes of *White Crucifixion* follow a circular rhythm about the central crucifixion; only the Cross, lit by a shaft of luminous light, and within it the seven-branched candelabra, create an area of relative stillness. A stony whiteness envelopes the canvas, bringing together the various elements of a single catastrophe.

Time is a River Without Banks, 1930/39

A first version of this painting shows that as early as 1930 Chagall was fascinated by the strange conjunction of a clock and a winged fish, flying over a river. The violin and the lovers on the river bank are later additions.

The oddly juxtaposed symbols derive from the free association of ideas, and are not therefore susceptible to rational explanation. The title seems to hint at a meaning, but a clock flying through the air – demonstrating, quite literally, that time flies – could give rise to any number of different interpretations. Especially as we know that the title post-dated the image, whose importance to Chagall is reflected in the way it dominates the canvas, emphasizing its significance. Here we are more or less in the realm of Surrealism, where disparate elements are brought together with dreamlike logic. What-ever Chagall's original poetic intentions may have been, the winged fish with its clock remains an image of curiously haunting resonance – 'an angel of the bizarre', to quote Edgar Allen Poe.

Scene Design for the Finale of the Ballet Aleko, 1942

Based on Pushkin's poem *The Gypsies, Aleko* is a ballet choreographed by Léonid Massine to music by Tchaikovsky. It is a romantic tale of a handsome young man from St Petersburg, called Aleko, who falls in love with Zemphira the gypsy; knowing their love to be impossible, he loses his reason and finally kills his beloved, so fulfilling his destiny as a wandering exile. Typically Russian in its sentimentality, *Aleko* could not but have its attractions for Chagall, and in 1941, while himself in exile in New York, he agreed to design scenery and costumes for the forthcoming production.

Here we see a sketch for the backdrop of the finale; Chagall responds only in the most generalized sense to the original story. Above the red of the earth stretches a stormy sky, in which a white horse with its chariot rises towards a bright yellow disc, suspended within which is the seven-branched Jewish candelabra. The image is one of a soul reaching up to find consolation from the suffering and pathos of life.

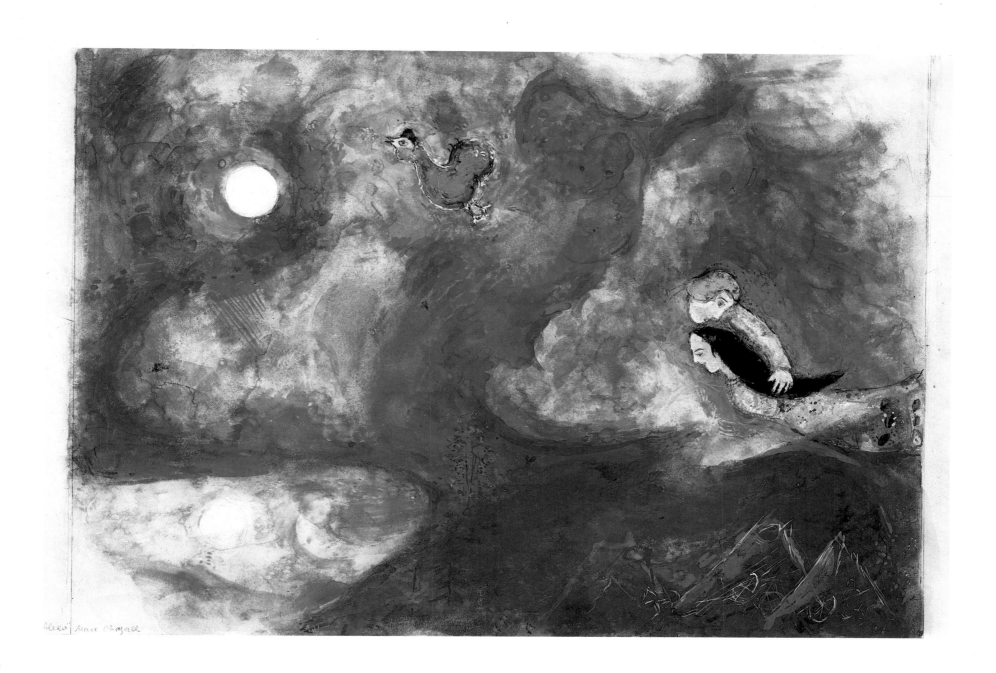

Flowering Feathers, 1943

'Ah Chagall's cocks, what would they get up to if there were no women? And their beaks, what beaks!', exclaimed Gaston Bachelard, the philosopher who wrote on the meaning of dreams. Here Chagall uses the creature as an image of female seductiveness, plump and rounded, adorned with a necklace, its feathers transformed into flowers. For by now the cock has made its appearance in Chagall's regular bestiary, along with the fish, the cow, the goat and the donkey – the latter often looking remarkably human, as he does here with his pair of male legs, and a desire to please that accords well with the biblical image of the patient, willing beast. The aggression of the bird's sharp beak and ruffled feathers is thus tempered by the good humour of the donkey, as he essays a few dance steps. No doubt there were some things Chagall preferred to express through the device of the animal world.

To My Wife, 1933/44

The dating of this picture is explained by the fact that, while in the United States from 1941 to 1946, Chagall reworked a number of canvases started some years earlier. He had already completed a first version of *To My Wife*, together with a number of sketches, in 1933, in Paris. The main difference is that in the earlier version the various figures are contrasted sharply against the zones of colour, while here Chagall opts for a more diffuse lighting which unifies all the elements, allowing only the pale body of the nude to stand out.

1944 was the year Bella died, and this painting is like an anthology of Chagallian iconography, from the *Reclining Nude* of 1911 to the motif of the bridal couple, not excluding the houses of Vitebsk, the violinists, the clock from *Time is a River Without Banks* and, of course, the host of animals. Chagall also uses to effect the red-blue colour combination that is characteristic of much of his later work.

Bridges over the Seine, 1954

From Chagall's numerous views of Paris, painted in the fifties, there can be little doubt of the affection he felt for the French capital. His ties with Russia were no longer so close, indeed the country where his beloved Vitebsk now lay in ruins was effectively closed to him; and besides, he had found consolation in the West through his second marriage, to Valentine Brodsky. The townscape of Paris became the usual setting for his familiar characters. Meyer has said, 'the town is the meeting-point of the inner world and external reality'; and so it is, for we see innumerable bouquets of flowers, cocks, lovers, etc, floating in the skies over the Champ-de-Mars, Notre Dame, the Arc du Carrousel and the Place de la Concorde. This particular painting is an aerial view of the sleeping city, against which are set a mother and her child, enfolded in the wings of a cock, a cloven-hoofed donkey and a pair of lovers. The river divides the canvas into two distinct yet broadly complementary zones, each containing a human couple and an animal. On opposite banks, maternal love and loving desire stand watch over Paris as it sleeps under the night sky.

Stained glass window for the Synagogue of the Hadassah Medical Centre, Hebrew University, Jerusalem, 1960-62

Most of the public commissions which occupied Chagall from the fifties onwards were of a religious character. The first of these was his contribution to the church of Notre-Dame on the Plateau d'Assy, a veritable gallery of modern art in a sacred setting. The experience of working on the church alerted Chagall to the potential of new techniques, such as stained glass. Here was a way of using colour as the dominant element on a monumental scale, colour that could be metamorphosed, through the skill and expertise of a master craftsman, into light itself. As fundamental to the success of these operations as the artist, the director of the Ateliers Jacques Simon in Reims, Charles Marq, must share the credit for much of Chagall's stained glass, including the windows for Metz Cathedral and the Hadassah synagogue. A close relationship of mutual understanding and trust was established between the two men, enabling Marq faithfully to represent Chagall's plastic intentions. Using new procedures, he found ways of registering different tones on a single section of glass, thus freeing the design from the fragmentation imposed by the traditional lattice. In 1959, the Hadassah, an American organization of Zionist women's unions, asked Chagall to decorate the synagogue of the university clinic on the hills outside Jerusalem. The artist chose to use the twelve large windows (340 × 250 cm) to represent the twelve tribes of Israel. Respecting the religious proscription against representations of the human figure, he found his imagery in the animals and plants of the natural world and in religious symbols. Biblical references to the twelve sons of Jacob guided him in his choice of a predominant tonality for each tribe – blue, yellow, red and green, divided equally among the twelve, and corresponding to the four sides of the lantern in which the glass is set, lighting the space from above. The synagogue was consecrated in 1962. Chagall's windows represent the summit of achievement in contemporary stained glass, his astonishing colours dematerializing into pure, elemental light. Not only do the Hadassah windows celebrate the people of Israel, they are also a hymn to the creative powers of art.

Ceiling of the Paris Opéra , 1964

In 1964, the French Minister of Culture André Malraux, asked Chagall to decorate the ceiling of the Paris Opéra. After some hesitation, because of the sheer scale of the project, he agreed. The approach he eventually adopted was to divide the area of 220 square metres into five differently coloured zones, each dedicated to two famous composers, shown accompanied by characters from their works. The scheme is as follows: red for Ravel and Stravinsky – the latter supplying Chagall with all the excuse he needed to paint Russian scenes, and to include a portrait of himself at work; white (streaked with yellow) for Rameau and Debussy; green for Berlioz and Wagner; blue for Musorgsky – who appears as an icon, surrounded by the chorus from *Boris Godunov* – and Mozart, shown with the magic flute from his opera; and, finally, yellow for Tchaikovsky and Adam, appearing with the dancers from the ballet *Gisèle*. In the small central area of the dome, around the chandelier, are grouped Beethoven, Gluck, Bizet and Verdi.

As we can see, Chagall chose to place the emphasis on French opera and ballet. The figures seem to be in motion around the circular ceiling, so that to all appearances they hang suspended in the air, like echoes of the melodies rising up from the stage. Chagall loved the theme of floating, and decorating the ceiling of the Opéra was as near as he could come to painting the sky itself; it inspired him to produce a masterpiece. 'Up there, I wanted to reflect, as though in a mirror, a bouquet of the dreams and creations of actors and musicians, remembering the colours of the audience's clothes moving about below. To sing like a bird, without themes or method,' said Chagall at the inaugural performance, addressing those privileged to be present as Garnier's magnificent opera house was revealed, alive with the glory of the painter's coloured harmonies.

The Big Circus, 1968

Chagall loved painting circuses. For him they represented the eruption of the fantastic into the grey everyday world. Everything about them delighted him, whether it was the animals, the balancing acts or the bareback stunts. Or to put it another way, the circus was invested with exactly the mood of enchantment that characterized the world of his own imagination, where animals spoke and people disported themselves like acrobats. Which is no doubt why the theme continued to haunt him all his life, expressed in picture after picture, among them a gigantic canvas that dates from 1956 (its dimensions 150×310 cm), the painting illustrated here, dating from 1968, and *The Big Grey Circus* of 1975.

Here, however, the performance is interrupted by a curious train of events. An angel looks down at the crowd from the heights of the tent, and the Hand of God appears in the arc of a circle, making a gesture of benediction, just as it is represented in the Byzantine tradition. And, finally, in a strange reversal of above and below, a horse's head reaches down towards a cock with a horse's body, ridden by a violinist. If the transformations of the figures are slightly perplexing, the distribution of the colours makes it clear that the various sequences are to be read separately, after the fashion of icons. The dominant black and white stands out with particular force since the bright colours are relegated to the edges of the canvas, like curtains that have been pulled aside to reveal the Divine presence presiding over the microcosm of the circus.

Flowers and Fruit by the Window, 1975

Although Chagall painted innumerable bunches of flowers, these are rarely still-lifes. Normally the scene is illuminated by some presence, some look, revealing the bouquet as an object of wonderment and delight. So here, in their abundance and brilliance of colour, the flowers and fruit are transpositions of the heightened emotions and fulfilment of love. Further, the motif on the tablecloth is picked up in the girl's skirt, and her blouse is as red as one of the fruits – as though the couple's happiness is itself one of the gifts of nature.

Sun over the Village, 1980

This sparkling gouache breathes a sense of sheer *joie de vivre*. The couple are in harmony with their universe, borne along by a patently good-natured cock, their loving conjunction echoed by the sun and moon that together illuminate the earth, united in a kind of cabalistic symbol. Here space is disposed with perfect rationality – there is none of the confusion of above and below or the wild distortion of which Chagall was so fond. There are three distinct zones: in the foreground, the couple and their strange mount, then the group of houses, and the sky, filled with representatives of Chagall's fantasy world. The darker mass of the village in the centre of the composition contrasts with the illuminated areas of the sky and fields, giving a wonderful freshness and spontaneity to a work painted by a perennially youthful artist of ninety-three.

SELECT BIBLIOGRAPHY

Monographs on Marc Chagall
CHAGALL, Marc. *My Life*, translated by D. Williams, P. Owen, London, 1985.
BACHELARD, G. *Introduction à la Bible de Chagall*, Verve, Paris, 1960.
COMPTON, S. *Chagall*, Weidenfeld and Nicholson, London, 1985.
HAFTMANN, W. *Chagall*, Thames and Hudson, London, 1985.
HAGGARD, V. *My Life with Chagall*, Hale, London, 1987.
WERNER, A. *Chagall*, Phaidon, London, 1984.

Exhibition Catalogues
Marc Chagall, Œuvres sur papier, Centre Georges Pompidou, Paris, 1984.
Chagall, Royal Academy of Arts, London, 1985.

General Works
ARGAN, G. *L'arte moderna 1770-1970*, Florence, 1970.
CHAMPARNAUD, F. *Révolution et contre-révolution culturelles en U.R.S.S.*, Paris, 1975.
LEBEL, R. *Paris-New York et retour avec Marcel Duchamp, dada et le surréalisme*, Centre Georges Pompidou, Paris, 1977.
MANDEL, A. *La vie quotidienne des juifs hassidiques*, Paris, 1974.
MARCADÉ, V. *L'art pictural russe*, Lausanne, 1971.
STRIGALEV, A. *L'art de propagande révolutionnaire*, Centre Georges Pompidou, Paris, 1979.
WIESEL, E. *Célébration hassidique*, Paris, 1972.
Catalogues du Centre Georges Pompidou, Paris: *Paris-Paris*, 1981 and *De Chirico*, 1983.

PHOTOGRAPH CREDITS

CHRONOLOGY

1887
Birth of Marc Chagall in Vitebsk (Russia) on 7 July.

1906
Studies at Pen's school of art.

1907
Goes to St. Petersburg where he enters the school of the Imperial Academy for the encouragement of the arts.

1908
Enters the Swanseva school, run by Léon Bakst.

1909
Makes the acquaintance of Bella Rosenfeld, his future wife.

1910
Leaves Russia for Paris with the aid of a grant offered by the patron Vinaver.

1911
Settles in La Ruche which is frequented by Modigliani, Soutine, Léger, Laurens, Archipenko.
Meets Max Jacob, Apollinaire, and enters into friendship with Blaise Cendrars.

1912
Exhibits at the Salon des Indépendants and the Salon d'Automne.
Apollinaire introduces Chagall to Herwarth Walden, director of the Berlin gallery Der Sturm and the review of the same name.

1914
First large one-man exhibition of Chagall at the gallery of Der Sturm in Berlin. Returns to Russia.

1915
Marries Bella in Vitebsk. Is employed in a war finance office in Petrograd in place of military service.
Meets the poets Alexander Blok, Yesenin, Mayakovsky and Pasternak. Exhibits at the Salon for the arts in Moscow.

1916
Birth of his daughter Ida.

1918
After the October Revolution, returns to Vitebsk where he is appointed commissioner for the fine arts.

1919
Founds the Free Academy. Among the teachers are: Jean Pougny, Lissitski, Malevitch and Pen.
Resigns after a disagreement with Malevitch.

1920
Leaves Vitebsk for Moscow.
Makes numerous sketches for the Jewish Arts Theatre.

1921
Teaches drawing in Malakhovska War Orphan Colony near Moscow.
Begins the compiling of his autobiography *My Life*.

1922
Decides to return to France. In the course of his travels, stops in Berlin where he tries in vain to recover his pictures left there a few years previously. Produces a series of etchings for his autobiography at the request of Cassirer.

1923
Settles down once more in Paris.
Vollard commissions him to illustrate Gogol's *Dead Souls*.

1924
Meets Sonia and Robert Delaunay, Marcoussis, Juan Gris.
First retrospective exhibition in Paris, at the Barbazange-Hodebert gallery.
Makes the acquaintance of André Malraux.
1926
Vollard commissions him to illustrate La Fontaine's *Fables*.
Chagall produces about a hundred gouache pictures as preparation for the work which will be realized in engravings on copper.
1927
Enters into a contract at Bernheim junior's.
Makes the acquaintance of Jean Paulhan.
1928
Begins engravings for the *Fables*.
His autobiography is translated into French and will be published in 1931.
1930
Vollard commissions him to illustrate the Bible.
1931
Journeys to Egypt and Palestine.
1933
Journey to Holland where he studies Rembrandt. Journeys to Italy, England and Spain. Retrospective at the Museum of Basle.
1935
Journey to Poland.
1937
Adopts French nationality.
1939
Winner of the Carnegie Prize.
1941
At the invitation of New York's Museum of Modern Art he emigrates to the United States. Meets up again with Léger, Bernanos, Masson, Mondrian, André Breton. Meets Pierre Matisse who becomes his dealer.
1942
Journey to Mexico.
Decor and costumes for the ballet 'Aleko' (music by Tchaikovsky).
1944
Death of Bella.
1945
Decor and costumes for Stravinsky's 'Firebird'.
1946
Retrospective at New York's Museum of Modern Art and Chicago's Institute of Art.
1947
Returns to Paris.
Retrospective at the Musée national d'Art moderne in Paris, at the Stedelijk Museum in Amsterdam, at the Tate Gallery in London.
1948
Makes the acquaintance of Aimé Maeght who becomes his dealer in France.
First prize for engraving at the 24th Biennale in Venice.
1950
Settles in Vence. Produces his first ceramics.
Retrospective at Kunsthaus in Zurich, Kunsthalle in Berne.
1951
Exhibition in Israel which Chagall visits for the second time. First sculptures.

1952
Marries Valentine (Vava) Brodsky. Journey to Greece.
1953
Retrospective in Turin in the Palazzo Madama. Produces the preparatory gouaches for the illustration of Daphnis and Chloë which will be published by Tériade.
1954
Second journey to Greece.
Journey to Italy. Apprenticeship in glasswork at Murano.
1955
Begins the series of Biblical Message paintings which he will finish in 1966.
1956
Publication of the Bible (105 etchings by Chagall) by Tériade.
1957
Retrospective exhibition of his engraving work at the Bibliothèque nationale in Paris. Produces a ceramic, two bas-reliefs and two stained-glass windows for the church Notre-Dame-de-Toute Grâce on the plateau of Assy en Savoie.
1958
Decor and costumes for Maurice Ravel's Daphnis and Chloë for the Paris Opera.
Models for the stained-glass windows for the cathedral at Metz.
1959
Receives the title of doctor honoris causa from the University of Glasgow.
Retrospectives in Paris, Munich and Hamburg.
Honorary member of the American Academy of Arts and Letters.
1960
Models for the stained-glass windows for the synagogue of the Hadassah medical centre in Jerusalem. Mural for the foyer of the Frankfurt Theatre.
1963
Sketch for the ceiling of the Paris Opéra at the request of André Malraux, at that time the minister of culture.
1964
Journey to New York.
Model for the stained-glass windows for the monument to the memory of Dag Hammarskjöld at the United Nations headquarters in New York.
Unveiling of the ceiling for the Paris Opéra.
1965
Mural paintings for the new Metropolitan Opera of New York.
Decor and costumes for Mozart's Magic Flute in New York.
1966
Settles in Saint-Paul-de-Vence.
1967
Retrospective in Zurich and Cologne for his eightieth birthday.
Exhibition of the 'Biblical Message' in the Musée du Louvre.
Tribute to Chagall, at the Maeght foundation, Saint-Paul-de-Vence.
1968
Journey to Washington. Exhibition at the Pierre Matisse gallery in New York.
1969
Lays the first stone of the Biblical Message foundation in Nice.
Travels to Israel for the unveiling of the Gobelins tapestries in the Knesset in Jerusalem.

1970
Unveiling of the stained-glass windows for the Fraumunster church in Zurich.
Tribute to Chagall, at the Grand Palais in Paris.
1972
Begins work on a large mosaic for the First National City Bank of Chicago.
1973
Opening of the Musée national du Message biblique Marc Chagall in Nice.
1975
Model of the stained-glass window for the Chapelle des Pénitents in Strasbourg.
1977
Exhibition at the Musée du Louvre.
Journey to Israel where he is appointed citizen of honour of the City of Jerusalem.
1984
Exhibition Chagall, Oeuvres sur Papier at the Centre Georges Pompidou in Paris.
1985
Death of Marc Chagall on 29 March in Saint-Paul-de-Vence.

LIST OF PLATES

6: Chagall as a young man.

9: Apollinaire and Chagall, 1910-1911, gouache.

13: A rabbi at the beginning of this century.

15: Chagall, *The Painter before the Cathedral of Vitebsk,* 1911, pencil, pen and black ink, 17.1 × 23 cm.
Private collection.

18: Chagall teaching in the Malakhovska War Orphan Colony near Moscow in 1921.

20: Chagall and the committee members of the Vitebsk Academy in 1919.

22: Chagall, *Study,* 1918, ink, 24.8 × 34.2 cm.
Private collection.
Chagall, *Man with Lamp,* 1921, ink, 46.8 × 34 cm.
Private collection.

23: Chagall, *Movement,* 1921, ink, 46.9 × 34 cm.
Private collection.
Chagall, *Abduction,* 1920, ink, 34 × 47 cm.
Private collection.

25: Chagall preparing the sketch for *Introduction to the Jewish Theatre*.

26: Chagall and his family in 1923-1924 in the studio on the Avenue d'Orléans in Paris.

29: Chagall, illustration for Gogol's *Dead Souls,* published in 1949.
Bibliothèque nationale, Paris.

32: Chagall at work on the portrait *Bella in Green* in 1934.

34: New York in 1942, front row from left to right:
Matta Echaurren, Ossip Zadkine, Yves Tanguy,
Max Ernst, Marc Chagall, Fernand Léger;
back row from left to right:
André Breton, Piet Mondrian, André Masson,
Amédée Ozenfant, Jacques Lipchitz, Pavel Tchelitchew,
Kurt Seligmann, Eugene Berman.

36/37: Chagall in Vence in 1958.

38: Chagall preparing the sketch for the ceiling of the Opéra, Vence, 1963.

40: Chagall touching up the Opéra ceiling, Paris, 1965.

45: *My Fiancée with Black Gloves,* 1909, oil on canvas, 88×65 cm.
Kunstmuseum, Basle.

47: *The Studio,* 1910, oil on canvas, 60×73 cm.
Private collection.

49: *The Model,* 1910, oil on canvas, 62×51.5 cm.
Private collection.

51: *Head with Halo,* 1911, gouache on brown paper remounted on canvas, 20.5×18.5 cm.
Private collection.

53: *The Drunkard,* 1911-1912, oil on canvas, 85×115 cm.
Private collection.

55: *To Russia, Asses, and Others,* 1911-1912, oil on canvas, 156×122 cm.
Musée nationale d'Art moderne, Centre Georges Pompidou, Paris.

57: *Homage to Apollinaire,* 1912, oil on canvas, 209×198 cm.
Stedelijk Van Abbe Museum, Eindhoven.

59: *Adam and Eve,* 1912, oil on canvas, 160.5×109 cm.
Saint-Louis Art Museum, Missouri.

61: *The Pinch of Snuff,* 1912, oil on canvas, 132×93 cm.
Private collection.

63: *Self-Portrait with Seven Fingers,* 1912-1913, oil on canvas, 132×93 cm.
Stedelijk Museum, Amsterdam.

65: *Paris through the Window,* 1913, oil on canvas, 132.7×39.2 cm.
Solomon R. Guggenheim Museum, New York.

67: *Over Vitebsk,* 1914, oil on cardboard with canvas backing, 73×92.5 cm.
The Art Gallery of Ontario, Toronto.

69: *The Jew in Black and White,* 1914, oil on cardboard with canvas backing, 100×80.5 cm.
Private collection.

71: *Feast Day,* 1914, oil on canvas, 100×80.5 cm.
Kunstsammlung Nordrhein-Westfalen, Düsseldorf.

73: *Jew in Green,* 1914, oil on cardboard, 100×80 cm.
Private collection.

75: *The Birthday,* 1915, oil on cardboard, 80.6×99.7 cm.
Museum of Modern Art, New York.

77: *The Reclining Poet,* 1915, oil on cardboard, 77×77.5 cm.

The Tate Gallery, London.

79: *Window in the Country,* 1915, oil on cardboard, 100×80.5 cm.
Tretiakov State Gallery, Moscow.

81: *The Mirror,* 1915, oil on canvas, 100×81 cm.
Russian State Museum, Leningrad.

83: *The Grey House,* 1917, oil on canvas, 68×74 cm.
Collection Thyssen-Bornemisza, Lugano, Switzerland.

85: *The Cemetery Gate,* 1917, oil on canvas, 87×68.5 cm.
Musée nationale d'Art moderne, Centre Georges Pompidou, Paris.

87: *Composition with Circles and Goat,* 1917, oil on cardboard, 16.5×23.5 cm.
Private collection.

89: *The Promenade,* 1917, oil on canvas, 170×163.5 cm.
Russian State Museum, Leningrad.

91: *Above the Town,* 1917-1918, oil on canvas, 233×136 cm.
Tretiakov State Gallery, Moscow.

93: *Double Portrait with Wineglass,* 1917-1918, oil on canvas, 233×136 cm.
Musée nationale d'Art moderne, Centre Georges Pompidou, Paris.

95: *Cubist Landscape,* 1919, oil on canvas, 100×59 cm.
Musée nationale d'Art moderne, Centre Georges Pompidou, Paris.

97: *Introduction to the Jewish Theatre,* 1920, sketch, pencil and gouache on beige paper, 17.5×48 cm.; squaring of the sketch, pencil, black ink and traces of watercolour on brown paper with squaring in pencil. 18×48 cm.
Private collection.

99: *Collage,* 1921, pencil, pen and ink, paper cut up and stuck on, 34.2×27.9 cm.
Private collection.

101: *The Window on the Island of Bréhat,* 1924, oil on canvas, 98×72 cm.
Kunsthaus, Zurich.

103: *The Lion Grown Old,* 1926-1927, gouache on paper, 48×40.5 cm.
Private collection.

105: *The Dream,* 1927, oil on canvas, 81×100 cm.
Musée d'Art moderne de la Ville de Paris.